Beyond the Corner Office

Essays by *NineWomen*

Judith Scheffler, Editor

Margaret Ann Chappell
Dana Becker Dunn
Fran Henig
Pam Hufnagel
Carol Knauff
Duffy Kopriva
Kathy Meier
Judith Scheffler
Yvonne Shepard

ISBN: 1-4140-2897-0 (ebook)
ISBN: 1-4140-2896-2 (Paperback)

This book is printed on acid free paper.

Designed by Fran Henig

1st Books rev. – 12/05/03

We want to first express our appreciation to our husbands and families. They supported us in our careers, put up with us as we laughed and moaned our way through multiple drafts of this book, and continue to encourage us as we explore Act II of our lives.

We extend our thanks to the many mentors whose doors were open when we needed sage advice and salute the women in the work force who went before us and set the bar, those who were with us in our efforts to improve business life for women, and the women who today are continuing to be a force for positive change.

Table of Contents

Introduction

We are nine former corporate women, averaging 54 years old. Active and energetic, too young to *really* be retired, we wanted to have fun, make money, and give something back to a society that had done so well by us. We wanted to see whether we could combine the talents and capabilities we had demonstrated in our successful business careers to create a more enriching post-corporate life.

We met for the first time in January, 2002, in a rented conference room in Bedminster, New Jersey, brought together by Yvonne Shepard, a former President and COO of AT&T Puerto Rico. Yvonne, a couple of years after her own retirement and at the conclusion of a consulting assignment in Latin America, was trying to figure out just what she should be doing next. She looked around at other women she knew who were in the same situation, and thought about the combined creativity and skills that were, in some sense, going to waste. She wondered if by joining forces, we could do something interesting and challenging, and *make a difference.*

The nine women she asked to join the group didn't all know each other, but we had something in common. We had all worked for some branch of AT&T for much of our careers, and had achieved considerable success. In the group was one of Lucent Technology's few female Distinguished Members of Technical Staff, six former Vice Presidents of AT&T or one of its spinoffs, and two former Division Managers. We had managed organizations that ranged from a handful of people to thousands. Our areas of expertise were widespread. We had worked in sales, marketing, operations, R&D, business strategy and information technology. One of us had been an officer in a startup in Texas after her retirement. Another had succeeded as an entrepreneur, owning and managing three office suite franchises.

Most of us had joined the working world in the 1960's and 1970's, when the role of women in companies like AT&T – and in society at large – was dramatically changing. We had been foot soldiers in the feminist revolution. We didn't think of ourselves as pioneers, and we rarely had our names in newspapers, but we broke down barriers, and raised glass ceilings. And as our careers progressed, our expectations and our lives unfolded in ways very different from what we imagined as we were growing up.

On a personal note, and to answer the questions everyone seems to ask, we are all married, some of us for the second time. Three of us have children of our own, and four of us have stepchildren. Two of us raised stepchildren who were living with us.

Now, all but one of us has retired. Statistically, each of us has thirty-plus years ahead of her. Once more, we are living in a period of transition as we try to define the next stage of our lives, which we call Act II.

Yvonne's ideas struck a chord in all of us. While most of us were totally uninterested in getting back into the corporate world, we also weren't ready to devote our lives to playing golf and bridge. We had worked hard, and often resented the lack of balance that our jobs demanded, but we had also retired young, and felt ready to do something interesting and intellectually stimulating.

Nonetheless, we each came to the group with reservations about what it would mean and whether it would work. As you will read in the essays that follow, we each had some misgivings, but were open-minded.

Our interest piqued, we began meeting every two or three weeks. We explored business ideas, using the tools we had developed in our years in the business world. We came up with a wide range of potential projects, but quickly narrowed the list to those ideas that involved "women like us" – women over 50, women in transition, professional women – we purposely left the definition loose. By our third meeting we were amazed at how much we looked forward to coming to meetings.

Months later, we embarked on our first project, not quite knowing where it was going to lead us. It was called "Across the Generations" and the idea was to understand the issues and experiences of women of different generations, and to somehow share that information in a dialogue between the generations.

As a first step we created a questionnaire, which we decided to try out on ourselves. It took us almost six months. In the process, we shared our histories and our expectations, and the lessons we had (sometimes painfully) learned. We laughed a lot, bonded as a group and came to a much deeper understanding of our experiences and what had shaped them.

In addition to the work we were doing, we added activities designed for fun and new experiences. Most of us hadn't known each other prior to joining the group. We hiked and grilled clams on Fire Island and Long Beach Island, and explored our adopted state of New Jersey with a tour of Duke Gardens and an invited talk on the idiosyncrasies of New Jersey state and local government. We helped celebrate Carol's "Alumnae of the Year" award from Fairleigh Dickinson's Silberman College of Business. We shared books we were reading and celebrated individual accomplishments.

As we learned more about each other, and began to trust each other, we started embarking on activities that were more than social events, activities that took us way out of our comfort zones, and allowed us to explore our creative and intellectual potential. Only a few of us think of ourselves as having artistic "talent," but as a group we took a "Drawing on the Right Side of the Brain" workshop that challenged us to do something most of us didn't think we could do. And we were astounded at how much we could do, after only a few days of instruction. Only a couple of us think of ourselves as writers, but as a group, we've just published a book! These activities – a kind of intellectual and creative Outward Bound – did more than help us know each other better. The group has helped us go places where we would not go alone. We learned new things about ourselves. We have discovered that we can acquire and master new skills we never would have dreamed of. Mostly, we've become increasingly enthusiastic about the potential and possibilities in this next stage of our lives.

As we moved along, we started thinking about what makes this experience so enjoyable and stimulating for us. Part of the answer is that our activities are not primarily social. Nor have we formed a classic support group. We had brought together bright, active, achievement-oriented women to learn and grow and work together on projects, one or more of which might enable us to once again help change women's lives.

Which is not to say that we don't occasionally become dysfunctional. We are, after all, human, and we are nine women, each used to being the boss, now working together in a leaderless group with only the minimally required organizational structure. Every so often things become, uh, well, interesting. We'll talk about that in the essays that follow, too.

At some point we recognized that the group and the process we used had become an end in itself. As we met a couple of times a month for the last year and a half, we created new friendships, broadened our interests, and opened up to possibilities in our lives in ways that, once again, we didn't imagine when we began. We believe that we have inadvertently stumbled upon something valuable.

Since the beginning of time, women have worked together, for the good of their communities, and for themselves. The act of working together on something interesting and challenging, in a supportive environment, is hard to find in our often frenetic, compartmentalized society. We believe that one of the reasons this group has been so meaningful to us is that it addresses this very fundamental need.

Then we realized: if it is true that we have stumbled on something truly valuable, something that addresses a fundamental need, we should share our discoveries with other women, ask them to join us, perhaps create a truly powerful network. Big ideas! Yes. But that's how we've lived our lives already, and our experiences in the group over the last year have taught us that we can do more than we ever believed we could do.

When Yvonne brought us together, she had called our group the "Brain Trust." We laughed, were intrigued, and accepted the idea that we would use our minds to solve problems. As time went on, we became increasingly aware that we are just a small segment of the community of women that has been working to mold a fulfilling and enjoyable place in the world for generations. We renamed ourselves *NineWomen*.

We decided that the best way to share our excitement about the group was to let our readers experience it through our eyes. Each of our experiences as part of the group was different, influenced by our individual personality, our history and our current situation. The body of this book is a collection of essays in which each of us describes who we are before we came together as a group, our feelings about being in the group, and what's next on the horizon.

We strongly believe that other women – in situations similar to ours or in very different situations – would enjoy the benefits of group membership. Our focus has been on women in transition, and, particularly, on professional women in retirement. However, we think that groups like ours would be valuable to women going through other transitions – women whose children are just coming of age or going off to college and who are trying to figure out what they should be doing next, women who themselves are just leaving college and entering the business world, women making career changes, women finding themselves alone for the first time in their lives.

So we are providing resource material for others who are interested in forming groups of their own. In the Resources section of this book we look back at the processes we followed and the lessons we learned along the way about what worked and what didn't work for us. We have also included a copy of our questionnaire.

We would love to hear from people who do form groups. We will be happy to provide any advice and support we can. We are looking forward to hearing your stories. And we are also interested in working with other groups as we create a dialogue across the generations and explore other projects.

You can contact us, via email, at NineWomen@att.net.

Introducing *NineWomen*:

Yvonne Shepard, group founder and guiding spirit: former President and COO of AT&T Puerto Rico, heads a consulting firm, married, avid golfer.

Margaret Ann Chappell, former Distinguished Member, Technical Staff, Lucent Technologies. Avid technologist, photographer. Married. One stepson.

Dana Becker Dunn, former officer of AT&T, Lucent Technologies and Avaya. On Board of Directors of Advanta Corporation. Currently living in Ireland with husband and son Patrick. Her stepdaughter and two step-grandchildren live in Connecticut.

Fran Henig, former Division Manager at Bell Labs/AT&T. Married, with stepchildren and step-grandchildren. Botanical artist, freelance dinnerware designer. Our graphics editor.

Pam Hufnagel, recently returned to working world as Marketing VP, AT&T Wireless. Golf and tennis player.   Married with stepchildren, "mother" of poodle named Bailey.

Carol Knauff, former Officer of AT&T and former CEO of WorldWideWeb Networxs, a company publicly traded on NASDAQ. Married, mother of daughters Casey (Kathleen Caroline) and Shelly (Christine Michelle).   Active in hometown.

Duffy Kopriva, entrepreneur, prior owner of three executive suites in NJ and Fl. Formerly Division Manager, AT&T Marketing.   An avid environmentalist, writer, explorer. Married, with three stepchildren and three step-grandchildren.

Kathy Meier, former General Manager, Marketing of Lucent Technologies, and Vice President, Marketing of a Texas startup company. Married. Restoring her 1830's house.   Avid reader, photographer, library volunteer.

Judy Scheffler, former CIO VP, Lucent Technologies.   Married, mother of daughters, Kathryn and Beth, grandmother of Nicholas. Writer, Editor-in-Chief for this book.

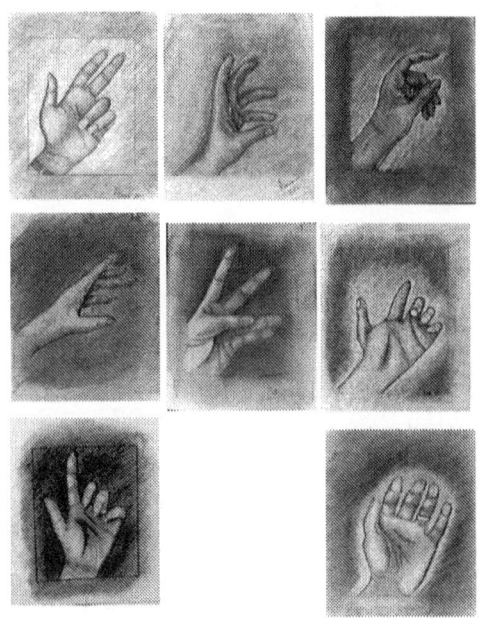

The Baby Belles in Act II

Judith Scheffler

    I entered a ladies room in the AT&T building where I worked and said "Hello." Three younger women, standing in front of sinks and mirrors, looked up, greeted me politely, quickly stuffed make-up and brushes into their purses, and walked out. Alone, I looked in the mirror. The forty-eight-year-old woman with short brown hair, high cheekbones, and dark circles showing under her eyeglasses who stared back

1

didn't look so frightening. The three ladies who'd left were among the thousand or so people who worked for me. They'd probably wanted to avoid having to make conversation. Or possibly they worried it would look like they were wasting time. Their actions made me feel like an outsider.

I never forgot that incident, perhaps because it was the first time I'd felt the isolation so deeply. It occurred in the mid-1990's when Lucent was being split off from AT&T and I'd been given an organization much larger than I'd previously had reporting to me. Though similar events happened often after that, I never got over my discomfort.

Seven years later I sat at a round table in a university banquet hall eating dinner with a group of women. We'd all either retired or taken a sabbatical. We were celebrating. Our friend Carol was being recognized by Fairleigh Dickinson University for her achievements at AT&T and her continued support of the university. Carol walked back to us from the head of the room, leaned into our table, and said to all of us, "For the first time I have my own inside group." The scene in the ladies room flashed back as if it had happened yesterday.

The "inside group" that Carol mentioned that evening consisted of nine women. All of us had been distinguished technologists or managers at AT&T, more than half of us had been executives or officers, and we'd all either retired or taken a package to leave AT&T or one of its spin-offs. We held our first meeting in January, 2002, agreeing that though we'd made significant contributions in the first act of our adult lives, we had a lot of spunk left and also wanted to "make a difference" in the second act. Not all of us at that first meeting felt we needed to figure out how we'd make a contribution as part of a group. That had been Yvonne's idea. We didn't even all know each other. Yvonne had picked us. Our ages ranged from forty to sixty. The youngest of us weren't ready to leave the business world and were checking out potential new positions, though there were few jobs available in the economically-challenged telecommunications field. The older members of our group had developed second careers, which were so far reducing rather than increasing our net worth, but which stretched our minds and allowed us to encourage our creativity.

Though many of us were skeptical about the group which Yvonne called "The Brain Trust," we'd all been deeply affected by 9/11. At our first meeting we considered whether there was anything we could do to improve the world situation. We soon decided we needed to choose a project that enabled us to take advantage of our areas of expertise. Developing a consensus wasn't going to be easy. Most of us were used to "running the show." At a later meeting Kathy suggested we use the "Post-It Approach." We all wrote six ideas, one per Post-It™, and placed them on a white wall. Together, not conversing, we walked along the wall moving the Post-Its around until similar ideas were grouped together. Kathy led us in naming those groups. Then we voted. The overwhelming winner: helping other women in transition. Some of us thought that meant sharing what we'd learned in our lives and careers. Fran led a project to design a set of open-ended questions that we planned to first respond to separately, then answer in our meetings, taking one question at a time. Perhaps we could figure out where to go from there. Designing the questionnaire, a stimulating project in itself, required several meetings.

Dana came up with the idea to hold a social event so the group could get to know each other better. In June, 2002 she invited everyone for an overnight at her summer house on Fire Island, one of the barrier islands along the New

York coast. When the group arrived, there was no running water in the house. Dana quickly arranged to have a plumber do a "quick fix" to enable the women to make it through the night. The rest of the group hiked up the beach to a small village to buy fish and clams and have a drink. The next day the group took a walk to a sunken forest on the island, planning to take a water taxi back, but the taxi had stopped running. The walk back seemed a lot longer. Despite the problems, the camaraderie made everyone feel closer. Due to other commitments I couldn't attend the event and worried that my absence would make me an outsider. Instead, at the next meeting everyone told me the stories and drew me in.

We started going around the table to answer one section of the questionnaire at a time in a July meeting. One of the early questions was, "In what ways did your mother's life-history influence your own?" Perhaps that was when we first realized how many similarities we were going to find in our lives. "My mother wasn't the baker or the cozy person," Yvonne said, "She was always a business woman and our main provider." Pam's mother thought education was important, urged her "not to get married too early, but to first develop a career." Fran said,

"My mother wasn't a warm, nurturing person. Her best years were the early ones when she was running a dress shop in Manhattan and some famous women were customers – she lit up when she talked about it." Margaret Ann told us, "My mother was the strong and willful one." Duffy said, "My mom was very strong and independent, and proud that she had a career before she got married." I told how my mother never forgave my grandmother for yanking her out of college after the first year because she'd gone to a dance with a boy. There was no money for my education, but my mother was so determined that in first grade I started working toward getting into college.

Most of us were pleased at how much our mothers pushed us. There was little resentment. Perhaps a wish that we'd had more nurturing lurked beneath the surface in some cases. Speaking for myself, I'd felt like my mother pulled back too far when I went to college, and later I wondered if her illness had caused her to retreat, or if she'd felt she'd done her job with my brother and me, there was little left for her, and just let herself slip into early senility.

Next we talked about how our fathers impacted our lives. We met two or three times a month.

"Maybe we'll be done by Christmas," Margaret Ann joked, when we realized how long we were taking just to complete our own questionnaire.

By early September the group felt we needed a break. Fran's avocation since retirement had become botanical art. Her work had been shown at several shows in the metropolitan area. The first course she'd taken had been "Drawing on the Right Side of the Brain" taught by Betty Edwards, author of the book of the same name. Since the trip to Fire Island, Fran had been promoting the idea that we all take a similar three-day course, given by an accredited instructor. Carol offered her home for the event. Art was not one of my participation sports. I would never have signed up for the event on my own, but the group's desires were both supportive and challenging.

The autumn weather cooperated and we were able to set up our drawing area outside on her deck. We all drew a picture of a cup and saucer the instructor placed on a table, but only Fran's actually looked like porcelain. Dana, who'd also been taking art courses, later produced a fantastic perspective drawing. Margaret Ann made us all laugh when her deck chair had outrageously long arms because she was determined that they should be their real length, not foreshortened as we see them. On the last day we each looked in a mirror and drew a portrait of ourselves. I was reasonably satisfied with the eyes and glasses I'd drawn, but the mouth I drew was a far cry from the one that appeared in the mirror. Yvonne's drawing came out like a good caricature of her face. Duffy, seeming naturally talented, drew a wonderful picture of her face and later worked on some additional pieces at home. Carol surprised herself and us by drawing incredibly accurate renderings of her cheeks and eyes and a good mouth. Having discovered a new talent, Carol began taking additional drawing courses. Not all of us wanted to be artists, but we did all want to zap the connections to imaginative neurons. I was proud of the portfolio of drawings I took home.

The group returned to the questionnaire. I mentioned the Brain Trust to a couple friends one night.

"Do you meet at your homes?" they asked.

"Oh no," I answered. "We rent rooms at a Corporate Headquarters Building. Our sessions usually last three hours."

"You mean you *pay* to sit at a big mahogany table like you used to do in business?" My friends were amused.

"It never occurred to me it was funny," I said. "And the table is oak." I was thinking of how the front-desk attendants kept asking our group why we laughed so much.

We weren't only determined to finish what we started when we returned to our meetings and the questionnaire that seemed to grow with time; we were coming up with revelations about our careers. So we kept at it. But Kathy insisted we take time out one day to bring in our drawings and hang them on the wall. She wanted to take some pictures with her new digital camera. Margaret Ann, who'd started taking courses in digital camera photography, shared her desire to photograph the event. The set of pictures we liked the most were drawings we'd each made of one of our hands. Our hands were surprisingly different in character, and all of us were astonished we'd done such a good job.

Margaret Ann changed her comment about how long it was taking to complete the questionnaire. "Maybe we'll be done by Easter," she said.

One of our more provocative discussions was about money. We had walked away from our companies when AT&T and Lucent were in their glory days, received pensions or packages, and cashed in a significant amount of our stock or stock options. Some of us were married to men who were still collecting a good salary. Yet most of us felt vulnerable. Why?

My lack of security stemmed from growing up with parents who'd lost all they had in the depression and had worked hard the rest of their lives just to maintain a modest standard of living. Some of us had done consulting after retirement for our old companies, bringing in extra money, but that was no longer possible. Our corporations were struggling to make financial numbers that would barely allow them to survive until the crunch was over. Lucent, for example, had shed 54,000 employees in the previous two years. Newspapers had suggested the company might go bankrupt. We were concerned about keeping our medical insurance and pensions. For me, there was another concern. What had I done to deserve my lifestyle? Why should I believe I'd be able to keep it?

One day, while answering a question about our work life, we discovered that each of us had sometimes felt the pain and annoyance of being an outsider – sometimes when we were with people in our own organizations and sometimes when we were meeting with other managers, usually men. We weren't surprised to find out that other women in our group had the same feelings. We were amazed that every one of us had strong feelings about how the problem had affected our careers.

When Fairleigh Dickinson University decided to add Carol to a group of distinguished alumni to be honored because of their business accomplishments and continued interest in the university, she invited the Brain Trust as guests in addition to her family. Her comment that evening about it being the first time she'd had her own group of insiders had amused us because we'd recently discovered how each one of the group had felt like an outsider. I knew that I'd never again remember the event when I'd felt like an outsider in the ladies' room at work without also remembering the warm feeling I felt that November as our group enjoyed dinner in a room where the walls were filled with oil paintings of people from the genteel set in the late 1800's. Later, when Fran gave me a photo of Pam and me she'd taken at the dinner, I was amused by my unusually wide smile

We discovered many other themes that ran through our stories and Kathy agreed to chronicle them. They included: having a religious upbringing, starting our careers tentatively and then blossoming in our thirties, changing from early naiveté to later assuredness, dealing with the balance of family and career, needing to be personally satisfied with our competence in a new area before accepting others' views, figuring out the significance of mentors as we went up the corporate ladder, deciding to play a major role in support of women's freedom to succeed in business, becoming mentors to younger women, initially eschewing power but later embracing it. We didn't all subscribe to each topic, but the correlation of our feelings was often incredibly strong. Sometimes one of us would say something unforgettable, like Duffy telling us that the day came when she realized "she couldn't out-power men, so she'd have to out-think them."

We set aside time at the beginning of each meeting for each of us to give a short report about something going on in her life. Kathy was methodically cleaning her house, going from box to box, and room to room, something she'd never been able to do while she worked. It turned out that Margaret Ann was doing the same thing. Others decided to get on the bandwagon. It was as if we wanted to make our pasts tidy before moving forward.

Kathy also described her personal fitness activities. Pam, Margaret Ann, Dana, and Yvonne all had their own physical fitness programs. Yvonne and Dana had decided to walk sixty miles in three days as part of the Avon Breast Cancer Walk. They started getting in shape months in advance, eventually taking fourteen-mile hikes. The rest of the group encouraged them and gave money to the charity in support of Yvonne and Dana's efforts. When a couple thousand women had walked in a heavy downpour the whole first day of the cancer walk, the event was cancelled. Our group encouraged Yvonne and Dana to realize they had personally succeeded.

We still hadn't completed the questionnaire by the beginning of 2003, not because our conversations veered off the mark, but because there were so many incredible stories. We laughed about our confusion in the mini-skirt era and became angry talking about managers and peers who considered us "articulate," but had trouble believing we could manage a technical project.

In early February, we decided to take another break and thought we should explore New Jersey. Voting on a set of suggestions that Fran tabulated for us, we chose a visit to the Duke Gardens. The indoor gardens were a place to remember Doris Duke's history, consider botanical art, take photographs galore, and enjoy the beauty of spring before it arrived. Yvonne made reservations for us at an outstanding Thai restaurant. Afterwards, the email continued for days as we collectively shared what a joy it had been to visit such exotic places with people who had become more than friends. The Baby Belles, as Kathy now called us, had joined together in an appreciation of what our lives had been and become as we worked together to design what we now sometimes called Act II. Despite all the extra events, we completed the questionnaire before Easter.

We kept wondering what made our group work so well. Why did we all look forward to the meetings so much? What were we really doing? One day Duffy shared some information she'd discovered about a group called "Junto" which had been founded by Ben Franklin when he was in his twenties. Franklin's group met once a week to discuss current topics of the day. The goal of the group was to improve their minds as well as their fortunes. Along the way they made significant contributions to their community with innovative ideas. The group lasted forty years. A key component of their success was the camaraderie and the support they gave each other. Duffy said that in one year we women had cleaved together in a similar fashion. But forty years?

I suddenly realized that various subgroups among us had been working to support the feminist movement for thirty years. The friendship between Fran and me went back to the days we'd joined AT&T at a time when computers were just starting to be used extensively in business. We'd gone to special courses, delivered by professors from Stevens Institute of Technology, to teach us how to program computers. We were both among the women who survived the courses and were given promotions to Members of Technical Staff. Later, AT&T ran a set of seminars for executives to encourage them to give women a chance to thrive in their organizations. Fran and I were invited to those events to show how articulate we were and to convince the executives we were capable of successful long-term careers. We were invited to give talks at organizational meetings and developed a humorous chatter, calling ourselves

"Bob and Ray" based on the radio program of the same name.

Later, I was part of a team of women that devised the Adopt-a-Zero program. We'd call an executive on the phone, tell him he was a "zero" and we were going to help him get out of that cellar. "What do you mean?" the called man would ask. "You have zero women in management in your organization," we'd say. "If you invite us to first talk to you, then meet with some people in your organization, we'll change that." No one told us "no," and we got quite a few women promoted during that program.

Yvonne and Dana had met each other at the Midwest campus of Bell Labs. They'd worked within a group of women there who supported each other so successfully that Chicago's group of exuberant women developed a reputation throughout the company. Like the men in Franklin's Junto organization, we used innovative ideas to solve a community problem. Our community, AT&T, was big enough to make a difference.

When Yvonne decided to ask us one day why we'd agreed to join the Brain Trust, we all admitted how surprised we were at how well the group was working. We'd taken advantage of mentors and other women in business, but hadn't thought we'd need them in retirement. Some of us had been apprehensive, worried that there would be someone in the group who would annoy us, or feeling that we'd never liked clubs and we didn't know why we should join one now. Yet each of us admitted we enjoyed every other woman in our association and looked forward to the meetings. No one felt like an outsider. We knew dissent would emerge, but felt we could work our way through it.

We realized how much we wanted each other's company in the next installment of our lives. We hadn't known it until Yvonne had asked.

The day came when we knew we had stumbled onto something so good that we had to extend it to other women in our area, maybe to women across the country or throughout the world. We knew we were dreaming, and we were practical women. So we agreed we'd start with something feasible. We decided to write a book to encourage other women to form groups with a similar purpose. That was an endeavor we could handle. What would come would come – and maybe it would be as exciting as the first year of our group.

But as I thought about encouraging other women to form groups like ours, I was left with a question. We were offering a solution. But what was the problem?

Serendipity played a role in my thoughts. My husband and I had been watching the 406-minute Russian version of the film of Tolstoy's *War and Peace.* I felt there was some connection. Great writers usually tell a story to enable the understanding of an inherent truth. "If the will of man were free, that is, if every man could act as he chose, the whole of history would be a tissue of disconnected events," Tolstoy said in his epilogue.

It wasn't just that we needed to clean up the miscellanies of our past and stay healthy. We had to understand what had happened in Act I before moving to Act II. I suddenly knew that I wanted to differentiate between what had been my free will and what had been my accidental part in history. As Tolstoy also said in *War and Peace*, "Reason expresses the laws of necessity. Consciousness expresses the essence of free will. . . Only by uniting them do we get a clear conception of the life of man." What concerned me was how I got into management in the first place. Wasn't my promotion just a consequence of history in which there had been little application of my free will? Weren't my continued promotions fostered by the Feminist Movement?

There were many similarities; perhaps I should say "histories," in the lives of the women in our group. The oldest members of our group had entered the same arena (the Bell System) at a point in time when the explosion of computing and networking gave rise to new opportunities. Furthermore, at least in AT&T where we started our careers, computing was at first considered a methodical job that did not require a great mind. An executive once told me that preparing material for computers was "work more suitable for women." Today that seems preposterous, but in the 1960's computers were just making inroads in business. It was the same time period other women (Friedan et al) were fighting for women's rights.

In the 1970's a NOW manifesto called for equal pay for equal work. It was estimated that across our country women were being paid fifty-eight per cent of what men received for similar jobs. AT&T signed a $38M settlement, promising to end race and sex discrimination; in the halls of AT&T this was called the Consent Decree. Computers were more heavily used in business, the first personal computers were being built, and two Bell Labs researchers were bringing respect to the field by working on an advanced computer operating system they called UNIX.

And there I was, by some quirk of fate perhaps the only woman in Bell Labs who had an undergraduate degree in engineering (the field still most revered by many Bell Labs elder statesmen) and a graduate degree in computer science. I was offered a promotion to supervisor. Sure, I'd worked hard to be there, but it was just an incident of history that caused me to be offered that promotion at a time when there were very few female managers in Bell Labs and probably all of those were Ph.D.'s.

When I first expressed my concerns about history-versus-free will, Yvonne had asked for a discussion of the subject in a group meeting. Duffy said that she'd once read an opinion about Roosevelt. "Other men could have done what Roosevelt did if they'd been at the same place at the same time," she said. "But they would have had to be men who stepped up to the situation."

"That's right, Judy," other members of our group chimed in. "You did what was required at the time."

I felt good then, but later I remembered how tentatively I had stepped up to the situation.

I'd been astonished, even frightened, when my manager had asked whether I'd be interested in being a supervisor.

"Heavens, no!" I'd replied.

The idea of being a supervisor frightened me. I didn't know how to manage people. My husband worked at the same company and at the same level. How would he feel if I were a supervisor and he was still a Member of Technical Staff?

That night at home my husband and I discussed the situation. I was surprised how positive he was about my being able to do the job. If he had any qualms about the problems between us my promotion could create, he didn't show it. We agreed I should go for it.

"I've changed my mind," I told my manager the next morning. "I'd like to be considered for a supervisory position."

"I thought you'd reconsider," he said.

But fate intervened and I almost missed that opportunity. I discovered I was pregnant before the promotion had been completed and felt I had to tell my manager.

"I think we better hold off," he said.

Fate intervened again. I had a miscarriage. I'd really wanted that baby and I sobbed uncontrollably in the hospital. When I felt a little better, and my doctor came to my room, I asked him how soon I could go back to work.

"In a week," he answered, clearly pleased to see me interested in moving on.

While he was talking to my husband, I picked up the phone and called my manager at work.

"Is that promotion still open?" I asked. "I just had a miscarriage."

The two men in the hospital room looked at me in astonishment, then started to laugh. But in a month I'd been promoted and soon had my second daughter.

Though I didn't know it then, that promotion was only the beginning. I enjoyed being a manager and leading an organization to some form of achievement. More than anything, I was an "idea" person, but people seemed to like helping me make my ideas succeed. By the mid-1980's I'd reached another level of management and my career was still flourishing, but promotions were few. The worst moment of my life occurred. My husband told me he was leaving because I wasn't the girl he'd married.

Devastated, I existed for a year primarily on Xanax and yogurt, pinning my skirts at the waist to hold them up. Though I felt bad about what had happened to me, I felt even worse about the impact on my daughters. By the time another year had passed, I'd been promoted to executive, officially divorced, and remarried – in that order. Using a take-off on a favorite Emily Dickinson line: Parting is all we need of hell, but sometimes the only way to know ourselves.

Thinking back to the conversation with the women in our group, I was sure they'd rally around me, believing I stepped up, not only to my first promotion, but to accepting who I was. History had been significant, but I'd also exerted my "free will." I realized there was something else that Tolstoy had emphasized in *War and Peace*. In the relationship between Prince Andrei and Pierre, he'd shown how sharing your deepest thoughts with good friends can help you understand how you fit into a broader whole. Eight good friends and the workings of our group had helped me feel good about my minute place in history.

But that was just my problem. Others of the women had different issues to resolve before we were ready to help other women form similar groups. Read on.

In the Beginning

Yvonne Shepard

Was it serendipity or celestine prophecy? Does it matter? Three years after my Act I, I was still on Intermission. Life was fine – lunching with friends, cleaning the attic, playing golf, starting a new workout routine. I filled my days with the things I'd always thought I wanted to do but never had the time to do. My busy schedule left little time to think about serious topics.

At night, when everything was quiet, I would lay awake and wonder if I was doing what

I was meant to do. You see, work and I have been good friends since I was very young. Born and raised in Puerto Rico in a single parent home where my mother worked very hard to provide the basic needs, I knew there was not much money left for non-essentials for my two sisters and me. There were many things I wanted, so I needed to figure out how to get them. In high school I worked after school and earned enough money to buy material and sew a new outfit that I wore to Mass almost every Sunday. During college I worked at the library and school cafeteria to supplement my college tuition. And after graduation, I worked at AT&T for over 30 years, often ten to twelve hours per day, six to seven days a week, so that it was sometimes hard to differentiate between my job and my life.

In early 1992, my vice-president called me into his office. Since this was not an everyday occurrence, I wondered what he wanted to discuss with me. I thought about all the possible things I could have done wrong. Did I miss a deadline? Did I forget to send in a report? Was there a mistake in information I had sent him? You should have seen my face when he made an offer that would give me one of the most wonderful experiences in my total work career!

He explained that AT&T needed to name a new President and Chief Operating Officer for one of its subsidiaries, AT&T of Puerto Rico, and the officers thought I would be the perfect candidate. Of course, there were some minor details that would need to be ironed out – I would be the first Puerto Rican and the first woman to hold this position. He explained that some people were nervous about taking this risk. He could take care of that. But, I was married, and he worried how my husband would react. What would be the impact to our marriage? Would he relocate with me to Puerto Rico? What about his job? I was not ready to answer those questions. I needed to discuss the opportunity with my husband. But I doubted that the company showed the same amount of concern for the wives and families of male executives.

After successfully undergoing a psychological examination, Ron and I convinced the company that our relationship could survive separation. I was to live in Puerto Rico and he'd stay in New Jersey. We would see each other for about 10 days out of the month when he would come down to stay in our Puerto Rico apartment. We were excited about the opportunities ahead for both of us. I would return to Puerto Rico in a position of significant power and influence and Ron's golf game could dramatically improve.

In 1992, AT&T of Puerto Rico was among the top 5 corporations on the island. I was a big fish in a small pond. As soon as word got out, I was deluged with well-wishers, flowers, requests for interviews, and long-lost relatives I did not know I had. Friends and acquaintances invited me to their homes and had welcome receptions in my honor. The governor sent a special welcome letter and my name was added to the VIP list of invitees for government and social functions. And then there was my family – my mother was bursting with pride, my aunts and uncles were very supportive, and my sisters wanted to help in any way they could.

On my first day of work, both of my sisters came to my mother's house for breakfast. I was wearing a navy blue linen dress, a single-strand pearl necklace, and navy blue low-heeled shoes – purposefully conservative. Anita, my older sister, gave me a hug that almost choked me, and then blurted, "You are dressed like a gringa!" She then promptly volunteered to go out shopping for more appropriate "Puerto Rican style" clothing. I tried to explain that this was more an issue of "dressing for the position" than nationality, but I did not convince her. She then pretended it was fine since she did not want to spoil my big day. When the time came to leave, all three of them – my mother, Anita, and my younger sister Olga – walked me to the car. It was all so special! It was all inebriating!

While overwhelmed and pleased by my reception, I also felt frightened. As I saw things, I was in a position to impact AT&T's earnings, the livelihood of the employees of AT&T of Puerto Rico, and the quality of telecommunications for all the people of Puerto Rico. At the top of the company, I could now make things happen. There would be no excuses. I suddenly realized there is a lot of truth to the expression, "It is lonely at the top."

There was so much to do! Major changes were needed in just about every part of the company. There were many obstacles.

Early on I had to deal with an obstructionist, an employee who took advantage of the knowledge that my term on the job would only be two to three years. Believing that he should have been chosen for my position, he tried to undermine my efforts. He would tell fellow employees, "this too shall pass" and encouraged them to pay lip service to the changes I was requesting since "she will be gone before you know it, and we will all still be here." When I heard about his "campaign," I retaliated with my own. While acknowledging my tenured assignment, I convinced them changes were necessary if AT&T was to continue the investments that would keep the company in Puerto Rico viable. The employees understood the business situation and accepted that one of my objectives was to keep their jobs. My pitch created unswerving loyalty to me and the efforts I was leading.

For my part, I made a commitment to the people of AT&T of Puerto Rico, to the people of Puerto Rico, and to my superiors at AT&T that I would do everything I could to make this a successful company. And that I did. For two and a half years, I worked tirelessly towards our goals. One day I went to the supermarket, and the store clerk asked me if I was the "Doña from AT&T." I then knew that I had succeeded in positioning AT&T as a household word.

In the summer of 1994, as I left for a promotion back in New Jersey, I was filled with pride in what we had accomplished. We had gained market share, grown revenues and profitability, forged partnerships with the labor union and with the local telephone company and kept employment levels. I'd become so involved that my life and my work were indistinguishable. And for this very unique and special experience I am forever thankful.

When in 1999 I looked towards the future, I wondered how long I could continue to live a satisfying life without the challenges I used to face at work and without the consequential financial and emotional rewards. My mind, body and ego were not ready to retire, yet I did not want to go back to the same old ways of working until I dropped each day. I wanted fun, exciting, giving, worthwhile and profitable projects – projects that would make a positive difference in someone else's life. And I wanted TIME to do WHAT I wanted to do WHEN I wanted to do it. Yes, I wanted it all! Why not?

Full of ideas of what to do … searching … looking for the "one" thing that would be unique and wonderful, I had too many ideas. Nothing jelled. No path was clear. A few ideas squeezed in between my daily activities, for example: *as baby boomers aged, many of them childless, who would watch out for their interests when they were ill and unable to speak for themselves? Could I do something to help the elderly? What was Homeland Security and what was at stake? Could I help to define it? Could I find a way to improve access to good education?*

Could I find a different way of approaching these problems?

Inertia took hold of me. These issues are so complex and far-reaching that while I understood the need, finding solutions was overwhelming. I was not motivated to put the time and effort needed to do the research required. And then, on September 11, 2001 the World Trade Center Twin Towers in New York City collapsed, and with them the lives and dreams of thousands were buried under mountains of rubble.

The uncertainty and frailty of our lives became real for me. No guarantee of time, no guarantee of safety, no guarantee of quality of life. While I knew this before September 11, I was now propelled into taking action.

An idea started to take shape. Many of the women I knew were extremely talented, with a proven track record of success in the business world. Many of them blazed trails by being first to break through the gender barriers at Bell Laboratories and AT&T. Their persistence and resilience were instrumental as they helped bring about changes that improved the quality of life for women at AT&T, in other businesses, and in society at large. During the 1970's, my friends and I were foot soldiers in the revolution that brought about new opportunities for women. We helped change the rules, attitudes and barriers to opportunity by obtaining our own credit cards, being free of the fear of unwanted pregnancy, attending graduate school, having a career, traveling on business with a male counterpart, and moving up the management ladder. We thought we could overcome just about any obstacle. And we did overcome many of them.

Would these women want to rekindle their trailblazing talents and help drive changes needed for the baby boomers to have a higher quality of life as we age? Many of my friends had ambition beyond Act I, but no firm commitment to an Act II. What if we could pool this talent and channel it, developing an Act II to address the issues I was considering? What if we could make this a profitable endeavor? What if we could define a new way of working that did not require 24 x 7 efforts? What if we could have fun while working for something that transcended us? I thought we could be awesome. The more I thought about it, I could see the possibility of our joining forces, much like we had done during the Feminist Movement of the 1970's. I could feel the energy within me rising; the power of such a group could take us to places none of us could go alone. We could make a difference.

In October, 2001, after having lunch with Margaret Ann, I was catapulted into action. Our lunch conversation had been an instant replay of the thoughts I had been having and validated the need to try something different. On my way back home I called Margaret Ann on my cell phone. I suggested that we form a group of women and that the purpose of the group be to find solutions to the issues we had been discussing at lunch. This group, which I originally named The Brain Trust, would have a profit motive along with the social goal that the group would choose. Did that make sense to her? "Yes!" she answered. That night I spoke with Duffy, my entrepreneur friend. What did she think of the idea? She liked it! As I thought who else to invite join the group, I considered all of my friends. In addition to diversity of thought, I looked for friends who had strong convictions, were open to new ideas and at a similar place in their quest for opportunities, and who would be willing to make a commitment to a project of the magnitude I was thinking about. And that is how I decided to call Fran, Judy, Kathy, Dana, Carol, and Pam.

Our first meeting was in January, 2002. Everyone knew me, and a few, but not all, of the other women and the one man. Only I knew Drew. I invited him to the first meeting because I did not know how to say "no" and did not want to hurt his feelings when he expressed interest in the group. Well, Fran took care of that! Halfway into the meeting she said, "I think this should be an all-woman group." At first, there was silence. We looked at each other and it felt as if Fran had read our minds. Then we heard emphatic agreement from Dana, then Kathy, and then everyone else. This was our first group decision and the process of our group working together had started.

We developed a set of principles. We would be a leaderless group, would meet every two to three weeks at a rented facility, and would create an environment where everyone felt free to express their thoughts. Disagreements on ideas would be expected and not personalized; we would create a project, and would have fun doing whatever we decided to do.

We decided to begin the meetings by taking turns sharing whatever was on our minds. We learned that Duffy enjoyed reading *The Tipping Point: How Little Things Can Make a Big Difference* by Malcolm Gladwell, a book about how fads develop. By the next meeting Margaret Ann and Dana had also read it. Fran had read

Julia Cameron's *The Artist's Way* and still followed some of its suggestions. While Judy couldn't get into doing the prescribed "morning pages," Kathy decided to follow the plan and enjoyed it tremendously. As we shared our thoughts, favorite books, funny experiences, and challenges faced, we discovered we had similar experiences and expectations. Slowly, we evolved a common knowledge base that created an environment where we felt supported, respected, listened to, challenged intellectually, and free to create.

I consider myself artistically challenged. When I was growing up, I relied on my sister's sense of art and beauty to choose my clothes. I married someone who has the ability to help me put colors and styles together in a way I love. So why did I agree when Fran suggested the group attend a drawing class?

Most of us felt vulnerable when we started our drawing class. I appeased my qualms by deciding that I took the class because other people in the Brain Trust wanted to go and I was supporting the group efforts. I wasn't willing to admit I wanted to be able to draw. I feared failure and its embarrassment. The purpose of the first exercise was to demonstrate that we could all draw if we could learn to view objects differently. The instructor asked us to copy a line drawing of Igor Stravinsky and gave us explicit rules on how to proceed. What if I failed? I was tentative; my perfectionist streak began to show. My eraser turned black, and soon held more ink than my drawing pad. The rest of the group finished their drawings and were chattering while I still worked furiously.

Such a disaster had never happened to me before! I was used to being one of the first to finish. I commanded my inner self to stop erasing and keep drawing. Finally our teacher said the time was up. I quickly drew the last lines and completed my first drawing. What a relief! But then I saw that, while my drawing could be improved, it did resemble Stravinsky. To my surprise, I was no longer afraid. I was still not certain I could learn to draw, but I was ready to try.

In three days, we went through a whirlwind course that took us all the way to doing a self-portrait. Mine turned out like a caricature and the group liked it. Fran and Dana did beautiful drawings, showcasing their talent for us. In fact, everyone in the group displayed a talent well beyond their expectations. My favorite activity was the drawing of our hands. Something special happened. I think there is a lot to be said about the personality of a person by looking at how they place their hands. After we finished we hung our pictures to show them to the rest of the group. I looked at the drawings and was able to figure whose hands they were mostly by how they were positioned. In the end we all enjoyed our accomplishments.

So there we were, a group of left-brain trained professionals learning to develop our right-brain talent. We had a great teacher, beautiful weather, and Carol's home provided the perfect site. Importantly, we gave each other great support and shared the joy of learning and discovery. This reinforced my belief that this group of individuals could accomplish whatever goals it set for itself.

One of our favorite projects was the questionnaire. It did not start as a project, but rather as a tool to be used for another activity that we called "the cross-generations project," intending to understand how women of different generations have and are coping with the issues we faced as women in business. The process of creating and testing the questionnaire took us into discussions about our values, difficult times in our lives, funny stories, and lessons learned. The interactions made us bond in a very powerful way. From the start I knew this was a special group of women, but my admiration for each and every one continued to grow. I learned about the poise with which Judy handled her life-transforming experiences, the perseverance and courage of Carol becoming the first one in her family to attend college, the blossoming of Fran's artistic talent in spite of so many years of it being repressed, and the creativity Duffy used in overcoming barriers. All these experiences were markers along the course as we moved forward to become powerful women in our Act II.

It is now September, 2003 – we have been meeting for almost two years – the group relationship is evolving and with it the trust we need to continue and create new possibilities for ourselves. It is like discovering a hidden treasure.

We have been on a path of discovery – both personal and with each other. At the personal level, we have gotten deeper understanding of our joyful and painful experiences and gained comfort with who we have blossomed into as individuals. With each other we have developed new bonds of friendship. We know each other, not just as other women who share a place in history, but as caring friends. And the best of it all is how we feel when we are together – creating, having fun, discussing our woes, and celebrating our successes. The

Brain Trust has improved the quality of the lives of the nine women who started it. And this is why we have created this book.

I believe this is a first step in a journey. The Feminist Revolution of the 1970's touched many lives and sparked many new paths for women. These same women are now facing a transition to a second or third act in their lives. A group like The Brain Trust can help make these transitions a fun, useful, and inspiring experience and thus make a dramatic difference in the quality of life of baby boomers as we age. The process we are using allows us to tap into everyone's talents and ideas. We do not have to do this alone; we can do this with others who share in our experiences and in our desires. Perhaps other career women, retired or on sabbatical, will form groups like ours and join our efforts in some way we have not yet defined. At the same time, this book can provide a perspective for the younger generation of women who are in the workforce and who, although under different circumstances, find themselves asking the same questions we have asked ourselves. As they read about how we dealt with their issues, we hope this will help them as well. This book is not about proposing answers but rather about proposing questions. The process we have used to get to our own answers is the key to the enjoyable journey.

As we complete our first project we will be moving on to new ones. I am not sure which one it will be, but I am confident it will take us in the direction of making changes in ourselves which in turn will cause changes in a larger context. That is the way the baby boomer generation has worked and I hope will continue to behave.

The projects we pursue will be a lively topic of discussion!

Remembering You

Carol Knauff

Mendham is a small town in northern New Jersey. Some people who live there have parents and grandparents and great-grandparents who spent their lives in houses nestled among the same oak-hickory forest. George Washington stayed there. The revolutionary troops spent their hardest winter of the war a few miles away.

Soldiers would bring their horses to the blacksmith in "Mend 'em" for new shoes.

The high school principle knows all 1120 students by name, and he never wants the high school to get so big that he can't remember the names. He knows siblings who have graduated and where they went to college. He knows most of the parents by name too. Most of the town turns out for Saturday football in the fall.

The teenagers say that living in Mendham is boring. There is nothing to do. My daughter Shelly tells me that there are drugs at the high school. The kids are indignant when the school brings the drug-sniffing dogs into the school, because it disrupts their routine and they can't get to their lockers to get their books. But these are good kids, and they know it. They know that I know it too. Most of them started out in kindergarten together, and have lived here their whole lives. I know them and I know their parents. We're not one of the leading families of the town. Both my husband Jeff and I were always too focused on our careers. But in this small town we know the families who make things happen.

The town has been good for us. Jeff and I (especially me) both spent so much time at work that it was good to know our kids weren't being exposed to too much evil. And, as much as I hate the gossip usually prevalent in small towns, it was comforting to know that someone would call me on the phone and let me know if my kid was getting into or causing trouble.

Jeff and I watched the goings on in the town with a detached interest. We watched who was elected to the school board and the township committee. We paid attention to fights over who would be superintendent and how big the school budget would be. We usually saw the same names. It was fun to read the next installment in the weekly paper.

In April, 2001 bad news spread through the town. A mother had committed suicide. She had four children, three boys and a girl. One son was a senior; the second, a sophomore; and the youngest, a freshman. The daughter was in the eighth grade. The second oldest son had been diagnosed with leukemia two years earlier. Under the leadership of one of the school board members and a close friend of the family, the town had rallied around them. Meals were planned, and volunteer schedules developed. All I could do was cook because work took up too much of my time.

Shelly and her friends didn't really know what to do about the funeral. I encouraged them to go. They agreed if I would go along.

The high school was crowded with cars and parents. The students were dressed in grays and blacks. Some teachers were behind a desk with list of students who had indicated that they would be leaving for the funeral. The teachers checked off names as the students left. Everyone's head was down. The students I knew greeted me with a weak smile.

The day was slightly damp. The sky was clouded. Tears were near the surface.

Hilltop Church sits on top of a hill overlooking most of Mendham. It's a small white church built on a corner in the road. The high school is off in the distance, separated from the church by about a quarter of a mile of farmland where sheep and cows graze. The small, well-tended cemetery flows down the hill from the church. Cars were parked for blocks around the church and people streamed into the small space. Teenagers looked around in bewilderment, hugged each other and cried. It was clear that the church would be too small to hold everyone.

I saw parents and acquaintances; they too had their heads down. We greeted each other

44

with nods and sorrow. Just about the whole town, high school and middle school were present.

The casket at the front of the church was closed. Next to it was a picture of a beautiful, vibrant young woman. The sounds of Sarah McLachlan filled the church with the haunting words of her song:

"I will remember you

Will you remember me?

Don't let you life pass you by

Weep not for the memories"

The family stood at the front of the church – the sons tall and straight next to their father and sister.

The oldest son delivered a eulogy. He was tall and strong, with a tight composure and a determined step. He spoke fondly of his mother and her gaiety and funniness. He said that he had always tried to be the one she counted on and that he hoped he had succeeded. He ended by saying: "You always said you wanted to be buried in Hilltop Cemetery because it was a beautiful place where you knew you'd find peace. I never realized it then, but I can see the cemetery from my classrooms. I'll be watching over you every day. I love you."

The second oldest son was next. He appeared strong and his voice was firm and deep. He spoke of the support his mother had given him through his illness and the courage she had given him to go on fighting.

And then the daughter spoke. She looked like a replica of her beautiful mother. Her voice was firm, but her eyes glistened. She spoke of their thirteen years together. "Those thirteen years were wonderful. I wish we'd had more," she said.

The casket was carried out to the gravesite, the mourners followed. At the end of the prayers, every one stepped up to place a handful of dirt into the grave. The students didn't want to leave.

Shelly, her friends and I left the cemetery. All that I could say was "it's so sad," which seemed like an inadequate understatement to everyone.

All this happened when I was at difficult time in my own life, and I began to identify with this mother. Work and family had always been the center of my life, which didn't leave much time for anything else. There were things I wasn't happy with, like being too plump. And, our older daughter, Casey, was asserting her independence. When she turned eighteen early in her senior year of high school, she really believed that she was an adult and could do adult things. Of course, Jeff and I persistently explained that one wasn't an adult until one could support oneself. But this fell on deaf ears. She purchased and smoked cigarettes. She and her friends would smoke in our driveway and leave cigarette butts scattered all over. Her friends would burn rubber on our quiet, country street and the neighbors would call the police.

But, even though this was traumatic, she didn't do drugs and she was going to college in the fall. Jeff and I had both worked hard, we were looking forward to the next years, and we felt financially secure. Retirement was a long way away in our minds.

In the fall of 1999, things seemed to be going well. Casey had enrolled at the University of South Carolina and she liked it there. Work was crazy, as usual. There were people jockeying for power, and nothing was easy because the business was in a bad position. I had a personal "hide and hold" strategy, which meant I was trying to be as helpful to everyone as possible. I was trying to not make waves. I needed two and a half years until a full pension at thirty years. In

September, 1999, my then-current boss gave me a retention package. I thought that this signaled that he valued my contribution and wanted me to stay.

Jeff and I would usually go to The Pub at The Black Horse Tavern, a local restaurant, on Friday night. Almost everyone in town went there, and we could count on running into someone we knew. Mendham had intimidated me when we first moved there. I was acutely aware of not looking the Mendham part. I was way too plumb, my nails weren't done, and my clothing was less than interesting. And, I definitely felt like an outsider because we weren't active in the community. But, now I had relaxed a bit.

I didn't mind going to the Pub and running into people we knew. I felt that our lives were under control.

Then in early October, I started to hear rumors about a major reduction in the number of Directors and Vice Presidents. I knew about the reduction of directors because I had an individual who worked for me who wanted to leave the company. I had been working with the Human Resources Director for our business unit to get the individual a severance package. The HR director told me to hang tight for a few weeks because she thought a severance offer was coming. The reduction of vice presidents was new to me, and I was concerned for my job. I knew that if I asked her directly about the vice president part she would clam up and tell me nothing.

So I went to someone else whom I knew would give me the straight scoop. I asked her about the rumors and she told me that they were absolutely true. She told me the details of the severance package. She also advised me to say nothing about it and to ask no one. She said, "The vultures are on the prey. If you even mention that you might be interested, your name will be put on the list. Now, you may want your name on the list. If you do, that's OK. Go ahead and say something. But, think about it carefully and make sure it's your decision. I'm leaving. I can't take it any more. I'll get this same package, even though I told them six months ago that I was out of here in April. Which is good, because this is a good package."

Now that I had some knowledge, I went to the HR director. I'd been thinking about the process that we would use to identify directors who would be asked to leave. This is always painful, but I'd been through this with her before. We'd done past downsizing at all levels using a merit approach. It took time, but it ultimately felt fair at the end of the process.

I knocked on the HR director's office door, and she asked me to come in. She's is a pleasant woman of about my age, fighting the same weight problems and children issues as me. I always thought that she was fair and worked hard to do the right thing. And, even though there was a little distance sometimes because of her position in Human Resources, we felt very comfortable with each other.

I sat down across from her and said, "I know that we're going to have a downsizing at the director level. When are you going to get the officers involved? Based on our previous experience, the merit process will take a few months. We'll need to get started soon."

She replied, "There is no 'we.' It won't be done based on merit. We don't need the officers involved."

I was shocked. "You're kidding, right?"

"No, I'm not. I talked it over with my people. We feel the merit approach is way too much work and my people don't want to do it."

"What do you mean, too much work? This is never a good experience, but it's far less arbitrary when it's done based on merit."

"You're forgetting that it's the HR people who facilitate all the rating and ranking sessions, and coordinate all the paper work. That's way too much work. But most important, when we do it based on merit, we also have to be able to legally defend our position."

"So, if you're not doing it on merit, how are you doing it?"

"We're going to eliminate jobs and the people who happen to be in them."

"And, who's going to pick the jobs that will be eliminated? Don't you need the officers for that?"

"No. Your boss has decided that he can do that himself."

My boss was the new head of our unit who had joined our company six months before from a company where he appeared to have been ousted in a merger. I had friends at that company. They told me to watch out for him. But he was now my boss, and in my hide-and-hold strategy, I was doing my best to make him look good. He was the one who gave me my retention package, so I felt that I was on "OK ground" with him.

But none of this meant that I trusted his judgment to do the right thing for either the business or the people. I knew that he would love the power of sitting in a room consulting with the HR director and his executive assistant, who also happened to be a woman. I could see him sitting there pondering their advice, and then taking a thick black pen and crossing off people's names with smug satisfaction at "doing the right thing." As this image flashed through my mind, I forgot my hide-and-hold strategy, and blurted out, "What? You're going to give our boss an organization chart and a thick black pen and let him do this himself?"

The HR director couldn't understand my concern. She said: "It really is in the best interest of the company to do it this way. It's a lot less work for everyone and far easier to defend legally. If you eliminate a job, the job's gone and it's straightforward. The decision is about the job, not about the people in the job."

I stated my opinion: "You know that he'll eliminate the wrong people."

"No he won't. His executive assistant and I will help him."

I shook my head, and walked out of her office. There was nothing I could do to stop the tidal wave. All I could do was to prepare people to give them as much advanced notice as I could. I knew which of the directors my boss didn't like, so I could anticipate the thick black pencil crossing through their names.

At least I could warn them about what might happen. I wasn't sure where he stood on me, but I didn't have a good feeling.

A few days before Christmas, my boss called me to his office. He told me that there was to be a down-sizing and that in advance of the down-sizing, he was giving out retention packages to a few people. One of those people worked for me, so my boss handed me their retention package so that I could give it to them.

I couldn't help myself. I had to know where I stood. The fact that there wasn't a retention package for me meant that at least he was considering putting my name on the list.

"I notice there isn't a retention package for me. What does that mean?"

"It doesn't mean anything at this point."

"Where do you stand on me? I'd really like to know. I don't want to be in suspense over Christmas."

"Your job will probably be eliminated."

"What about my people?"

"Major parts of your organization will be eliminated."

"What about the work? How will it get done?"

"I expect you to figure that out. But, I really don't have time to talk about this now. You can make an appointment and talk to me then."

I walked out of his office in shock. I'd been with this company for over twenty-nine years, and with one nod of his head, I was gone. There'd be a stiff penalty on my pension, because I hadn't made the thirty years and I was only fifty-one. I was currently reading a book about a woman whom the author described as "Fifty-one, too young to retire, but too old to change careers." I felt like a victim of a drive-by shooting.

I walked past the HR director's office on the way to mine. She said "hello" as I walked past. I stepped into the frame of her door and leaned my shoulder and head against the frame.

"My boss just told me that he's eliminating my job."

"Oh, Carol, what did you do? Nothing's been decided yet."

"I asked him."

"He must have decided right there when you asked him."

I shrugged my shoulders and said I'd see her later.

Fifteen months later I was at the funeral of a woman I hardly knew, but I felt like I knew her. Maybe she thought that she had her life under control, only to have it ripped away from her. Maybe she enjoyed going to The Pub too, before things happened. I still felt like a victim of a drive-by shooting fifteen months after I lost a stupid job. It seemed pretty frivolous in comparison. But I didn't want to go to The Pub any more, and I suspected she hadn't either.

That's the state of mind I was in when Yvonne approached me in the late summer of 2001. Yvonne and I had worked together many times. I respected Yvonne, but more important to me, I liked and trusted her. I was crazy about her energy. She said that she had this idea to form a group. She didn't really know where the group would be going, but she wanted the purpose of the group to be "have fun and make money."

Yvonne said that she knew everyone would soon be focused on the Thanksgiving and Christmas holidays, so she intended to wait until January to actually get started. She asked me if I'd be interested. I really didn't give it much thought. I just agreed because that was the easiest thing to do. Then I pretty much forgot about it.

True to her word, Yvonne convened the first meeting of the group in January, 2002. I missed the first few meetings for stupid reasons. My power went off and I couldn't get the garage door open. The music director from the high school told me he needed refreshments for 200 people the next day so I had to bake cookies instead of attending the meeting. Perhaps I was avoiding the meetings because I was afraid.

Indeed, at the first meeting I attended, I did exhibit signs of fear. I can remember sizing everyone up. I can't remember what I thought, but I do remember having my defensive walls up. I went to the meetings sporadically, as we worked our way through green-lighting sessions about what we might do for the "make money" part of our goal.

As we spent more time together, my walls started to come down a little. We spent a wonderful few days at Dana's on Fire Island. Then, we had a great experience at the class on "Drawing on the Right Side of the Brain." We got to spend quality time with each other working on something that was very new and different to some of us. I now felt like I had eight good friends.

But, I still hadn't really recovered from the blow of being forced out of my job, and my self-confidence was in shambles. I internalized everything, and really believed that the success I had achieved in those twenty-nine years had been a fluke. I felt like, after what was now fifty-three years, I had finally become what I was always destined to be – plump, old and unemployed. Having eight good friends helped, but I really wasn't doing much healing.

Then we started the questionnaire. Perhaps I missed too many meetings, or I'm experiencing early senility. I can't remember why we started the questionnaire. But I do remember the meeting when someone else started talking about how they felt like an imposter for most of their career. I think it might have been Dana who started the discussion. She said that she kept thinking that someone had made a mistake, and that she'd be found out. Then the whole group burst into discussion, saying that they had felt the same way.

That day I think that I really started to heal. As I heard others say the things that haunted me, I realized that my insecurities were fairly universal, and mostly inaccurate.

Outwardly, not much has changed about me, except that I'm now fifty five years old. But I'm a different person. I go to the Pub all the time now.

Post Script: It takes a long time to write. I first wrote this piece about six months ago. And, now, as I'm putting the final touches on it, I realize that a minor miracle has taken place for me. The minute I stepped into an engineering classroom in the summer of 1966 at Penn State University, I became an outsider and I stayed that way for thirty-five years. In 1966, there were only two women in the College of Engineering, Jane, in Chemical Engineering, and me, in Electrical Engineering. When I worked, especially in the beginning, it was me and the men. And, when I'd get to spend time with the wives of the men I worked with, I'd think: "Finally, I won't be an outsider." Then they would invariably ask me

"How can you leave your children?" and look at me as if I was some kind of strange mutant. Once again, I was on the outside.

Now I'm not an outsider any more. Our group was the first place that I realized this. But, I'm also an insider in every group in which I participate – the high school, the community, charitable organizations, friends, ladies who lunch, whatever. Part of the reason for this is that I am now doing things people expect me to do. I'm OK, I match behavior expectations, and I'm an insider. And, part of the reason is that I have more time to spend on being a part of the group. When I was the outsider, I always thought it was me. Maybe something was a little wrong with me – I was a few degrees out of phase, or maybe I really was a mutant. But now I know it wasn't me. I was trying to break through glass barriers. And, when I start behaving in counter-expectation ways again – and I will, trust me – I'm going to be a lot better at breaking those glass barriers because I will know it isn't me.

New Directions

Fran Henig

"Would you tell me, please, which way I ought to go from here?"

"That depends a good deal on where you want to get to," said the Cat.

Alice's Adventures in Wonderland, Chapter VI

Here I am, fifty-nine years old, and I have just received a check – my first – for two designs I have sold to a company that manufactures casual dinnerware for places like Macy's and Bloomingdale's. I don't know yet whether these designs will actually make it to the stores – that will depend on how many orders the manufacturer receives once they start showing the samples. And the money, compared to what I was earning at AT&T/Lucent or for the consulting work I did afterwards, is laughable. But the satisfaction of having achieved this milestone as a freelance artist, for my own creative designs, is just incredible.

There are people who have known exactly what they wanted to be "when they grew up" from the time they were five or six.

I am not one of them.

When I went to work for Bell Labs, it was not because I was fascinated by technology, or wow'ed by the prestigious Bell Labs name, or was setting out to demonstrate that women could be successful in non-traditional fields.

It was 1964. I had just graduated summa cum laude from Wheaton College in Massachusetts and I needed a job, since there were no marriage plans on the horizon. (A sign of the times all by itself.) I didn't seem to have any of the standard female nurturing genes that would support a career in teaching, nursing, or social work. I didn't have my father's business skills or my mother's fashion sense. And I was desperately afraid of public speaking.

Bell Labs, trying to hire people who could be trained to write software, offered me the highest salary in my graduating class, and the opportunity to get a master's degree in computer science going to school on company time two days a week, with tuition and books paid for by the company. I had never seen a computer.

I wish I could say that it was love at first sight. But it wasn't. I was not a natural with technology, and I was lonely and miserable those first few years as a single person in suburban New Jersey where everyone else seemed to be settled and married and very Republican.

But, since I couldn't figure out what else I could be doing, and this *was* a good job with a great salary, I "muddled through." And – much to my surprise – it all worked out.

Thirty-two years later, when I retired at the age of 52, I was proud of the career I had created. For the last thirteen years of my career I had been a Division Manager in the portion of AT&T that was soon to become Lucent Technologies. The organizations I led designed, developed and supported software systems to help local telephone companies and other telecommunications service providers run their operations. We developed systems to help customer service representatives handle and isolate customer telephone problems, and preventive maintenance systems to predict where network failures were going to occur. We developed and deployed some of the first commercial systems using a new technology called "Expert Systems," and at the same time, helped develop the Expert Systems technology itself. We worked closely with Bell Labs' research scientists, our customers, and the users in the field to apply leading edge technology to solve real business problems for our customers – and to make money for AT&T.

It was a very dynamic environment. The telecommunications industry was changing from a monopolistic Bell System into the global, highly competitive, and largely deregulated industry it is today. The company I had joined evolved from the R&D-oriented Bell Labs to the market- and bottom-line oriented organizations that ultimately formed Lucent Technologies. The computer and software technologies we were using changed at least as much – the large mainframe computers that were servicing thousands of people when I started work had less processing power than the average Palm Pilot does today.

And, last, but certainly not least, the role of women in the company, in the industry, and in society, was changing dramatically. When I was promoted to my first technical management job in 1971, I was one of eight female technical managers in all of Bell Labs. There were no women in any higher managerial rank in the technical ladder. Twenty-eight years later, Carly Fiorina left Lucent to be CEO of Hewlett-Packard, and, more recently, Pat Russo re-joined Lucent as its CEO. There were and are still lots of problems facing women in corporate America, but we had, indeed, come a long way.

On a personal level, during these years I met and married my husband, Ed, – a marriage that is the center of my life – and acquired good friends and many interests.

There was an old adage when I was a teenager that the party should end while everyone was still having fun. Ed retired from his "back office" Wall Street job in 1994, and I was, more than ever, struggling with the "balance" issue – balancing the demands of an all-consuming job with my personal life and all the other things that I wanted to do. AT&T helped out by offering an early retirement option, as part of an early round of downsizing the company prior to spinning off Lucent

Technologies and Avaya. Ed and I realized that we could pull this off financially, and I grabbed the opportunity.

So I left AT&T in 1996 feeling good about the people I had worked with, the organizations I had built and the products we had produced, the barriers I had broken and the positions I had achieved.

What I didn't have was a plan.

I left work thinking that I *might* want to do some graduate work in history, but having spent the last three decades living with deadlines and schedules, I needed to take a year off before I committed myself to an academic calendar. And I certainly wasn't ready to face GREs.

As a retirement present to myself, I signed up for a five-day, $1200 art class called "Drawing on the Right Side of the Brain," given by Betty Edwards in New York. Edwards believes that the ability to draw is not a God-given talent, but a skill that anyone can acquire. Her class focuses on getting rid of the self-consciousness we develop as adults, and turning off the left-brain, analytic selves that get in the way of our "seeing" what is actually in front of us, as opposed to seeing what we "know" is there.

I had enjoyed art as a child, but hadn't done much as I got older, and didn't think I had any talent. Nothing in my adult years challenged this belief; even my doodles seemed dull and uninspired. I had read Betty Edwards's book years earlier, and had found it intriguing. Perhaps, if I could learn to draw, art would be a nice retirement pastime.

The class itself was a bit of a disaster. It came in the middle of the January 1996 blizzard, and I missed two of the five days. Betty Edwards slipped on the ice and broke her wrist. I enjoyed the three days of the class that I managed to get to, but was by no means a star student. My drawings were mediocre and without clarity or form or personality. I looked at the work of my fellow students and shook my head at my lack of ability.

Nonetheless, taking art classes seemed like a pleasant enough way to spend some time – along with yoga, traveling and learning to play a bad game of golf – so I signed up for drawing and then painting classes at a local art center. Again, I enjoyed being in the classes, and occasionally produced something I liked, but I didn't feel like I knew what I was doing, or that I was getting any better.

A serendipitous comment from a fellow student at the local art center led me to the New York Botanical Garden (NYBG) in the Bronx. The NYBG has a comprehensive and renowned Botanical Art and Illustration program, which – amazingly – takes novices like me and offers rigorous instruction in everything from basic drawing to plant morphology, taught by some of the best practitioners in the field.

So now, seven years after I retired, I am a dues-paying member of the American Society of Botanical Illustrators and the Guild of Natural Science Illustrators, exhibiting my work in juried art shows and selling freelance china designs to the casual dinnerware market. I still shake my head at the work I do compared to what the "good" people in the field are doing, and I still have a lot to learn. But I find it totally engrossing.

I never could have imagined doing any of this.

Sometimes, it seems to me, you don't need a plan.

For all of us, I think, retirement is a time of exploration, experimentation, and self-discovery. This can be terrifying. When I retired I thought, *omigod*, what if I am totally bored after three months and spend all day watching soap operas and eating chocolate and getting fatter and fatter and more and more depressed? Except for the chocolate part, this hasn't turned out to be a problem. Instead, my problems are the same as they were when I was working: focus and time management. There are more things I want to do in any given day than I can possibly do; at the same time I am still really good at procrastinating about the things on my "have to" list.

When Yvonne asked me to participate in the group, I was flattered that these high-achieving women were interested in having me join them, but a little leery of yet another commitment. I had lost contact with Yvonne and Dana since the days we had worked together, and was looking forward to getting reacquainted with them. Judy and I had been friends since our early days at the Labs, and I had known Margaret Ann since she was one of my mentees during the 1980's. I'd never met Carol, Kathy, Duffy and Pam.

I had mixed feelings, too, about the business side of Yvonne's idea. In the years since I had retired, I had been lucky enough to fall into an ideal retirement job. I helped create and deliver training workshops for new managers, for both Lucent and AT&T. I ran over 50 workshops in five years, mostly in places like Piscataway, NJ and Columbus, OH, but occasionally in exotic locations, like Paris, Warsaw and Beijing. The work was both exhausting and stimulating; rewarding both financially and personally. It ended when the telecom boom ended in mid-2000, and I missed it. On the other hand, I wasn't ready to sign up for anything that looked or felt like a full-time job. I wanted time to play and to paint and to explore the possibilities of freelance design work.

Other members of the group were in different places. Pam was on the opposite end of the spectrum, and was actively looking for a "real job." Dana was in the early stages of retirement and clearly wanted to take advantage of this time to explore and play. Duffy was interested in doing something entrepreneurial. Margaret Ann was in that early panic state – What am I going to do with the rest of my life? Kathy was busy cleaning her attic – a stage I seem to have missed. Carol's priority was spending time with her daughters. We were all over the place, and it wasn't clear how seriously we were committed to this group of women, most of whom we didn't know.

The process of figuring out the purpose of the group pulled us together. Kathy led us through processes we had all been through a zillion times at work: we brainstormed ideas; then analyzed, categorized, and grouped them. We plastered Post-Its™ all over the walls of our rented conference room, and then multi-voted on the ideas that most interested us.

This time, however, these processes were a lot more fun. At work, our main driver had been the bottom line, and we had operated with strict deadlines, under a lot of pressure. Now we had the luxury of time and of not having to meet any quarterly corporate earning commitments. Nonetheless, as some of the suggestions went up on the conference room wall, I could feel myself recoil. Yes, we might make money brokering retired talent, or building homeland security systems, or helping senior women with healthcare referrals or financial planning – but did I *want* to do any of these things? If one of these had been chosen as our first project, I probably would have dropped out.

Surprisingly, we all seemed to have the same reaction. When the multi-voting was done, we had picked our first project based on where our interests and energies lay, not based on our best chances for a successful financial outcome. I was interested in capturing our history – the history of women like us, the "foot soldiers of the revolution" who weren't necessarily the initial pioneers or the big names, but the first generation of women to move up the corporate ladder in any significant numbers. We had lived through interesting times, and I was afraid that that experience and all our stories were going to get lost while the history books talked about the Gloria Steinems and the Betty Friedans. A conversation between Dana and Kathy broadened this idea into a project we called "Across the Generations," where our goal was to capture and share the issues and experiences of multiple generations of women.

How does this meet the objective of creating a profitable business? That wasn't (and still isn't) at all clear. We have some ideas on the subject, but to call them half-baked would be generous.

This is fine with me. It is the way I had been "managing" – *much* too generous a word – my retirement, and it is the way I like to work. I am a real believer in "organic development" – taking a seed idea and seeing where it will lead you, rather than following a defined path. More surprisingly, it doesn't seem to be a problem for the rest of the group; although periodically one or the other of us gets itchy and – rightly – starts asking questions about just where it is that we are headed.

Launching into our Across the Generations project, we prepared a questionnaire that would allow women to explore their backgrounds and parents' expectations, their experiences growing up and as women in the working world, and their hard-earned lessons and regrets. We decided to try it out on ourselves.

The questionnaire was only three pages long, but we discovered we could rarely get through more than a handful of questions in one of our three-hour meetings. The discussions were fascinating, and we couldn't stop talking. To an outside observer, we look a lot alike: we are all white, financially comfortable, married suburban women, and we all had worked for the same corporation for most of our careers. But as soon as that layer was peeled away the similarities and differences in our backgrounds and personalities began to shine through. Dana was from a strict Southern Baptist family, and in her early years moved around the country several times a year, as her father's job demanded. I was a "nice Jewish girl" from Queens, whose father had come from Europe before the Second World War. Margaret Ann was from a strict Catholic Ohio background, with a genealogical tie to Mormon founder Joseph Smith; Yvonne came from a divorced Puerto Rican family; Carol from a large

Italian family in Western Pennsylvania; and so forth. For many of us, our backgrounds were more humble than our current circumstances. We grew up having in common our families' expectations that we would get a college education and get married and have kids, although few of us did the last.

We were also lucky enough to live in an era of dramatically increasing opportunities for women. As we told our stories, it became apparent how much our success was dependent on the combination of our individual talents and the doors that were open to us because of Affirmative Action and the Consent Decree AT&T signed with the Justice Department in 1973, in response to gender discrimination charges by the FCC and the EEOC. Those of us in Bell Labs were barely aware of the Consent Decree, but were caught up in Affirmative Action programs and activities that increased our awareness of the issues facing women and minorities, spawned formal and informal support networks, and undoubtedly gave us greater exposure within the Corporation. Those working for AT&T at the time were given dramatic pay raises when the Consent Decree was signed, and then went through formal assessment programs that opened their eyes – and their managers' – to career opportunities and job assignments that otherwise would never have been available. The working world we had so naively entered was a different place. We had indeed lived through an historic time, and it had shaped each of our lives in different ways.

It took us almost six months to work our way through the questionnaire. Our stories had us laughing, gasping in recognition or astonishment, and occasionally getting choked up. The sheer range and, oh, humanness of our experiences created bonds between us that would have taken years to develop otherwise. This wasn't an intense group therapy session or one of those "charm school" group psychology sessions we occasionally had been through in workshops at work. It was fun; it was a celebration and a recalibration of our lives and our work experiences and where we were now. I looked forward to our meetings, and came out of each with my head full of stories and wonder. By the time we shared our last answers we were excited about the group and anxious to share the experience with others.

Finishing the questionnaire and then figuring out what to do with it and what do to next could have been a real downer, but it wasn't. Carol came up with the idea of capturing our stories and our experiences and the key lessons we had learned in what we affectionately called "The Bestseller." The idea of helping others create groups similar to ours had been floating around for a while and kept reappearing, and Judy came up with the idea of writing this book to both capture our own experiences and act as a "how to" guide to help others. Everybody seemed to glom onto this as our next project, possibly writing our Bestseller chapters in parallel. Margaret Ann started exploring what we would want or need in a web site. I came back from a ten-day vacation in Costa Rica to a flood of emails. Everybody was energized, lots of work was going on between meetings (we hadn't done much of that before) and we seemed to be finding a path forward just by putting one foot in front of the other and going with the energy. Everybody was ready to get down to work and do something concrete.

So it was a real shock when I came back from a concert one night about a week later, and, checking my email before I went to bed, picked up the following message:

Hi guys

Don't know how to say this to you, but today really sent me into a tailspin. I don't know how to figure out what happened.

> But, this hasn't bothered me so much in a
> long time. I think that I should resign from
> the group. I wish you the best.
>
> Carol

Now the meeting that day *had* been a bit of a mess. We had too much to cover to begin with, which was not unusual, and had gotten sidetracked, one more time, on "the big questions" (what is the business case, why can't we explain this to someone on an elevator? what is it we are and are not trying to do?). I said to Judy as we drove home, "My head is spinning. We were all over the place." Which we were. Nonetheless, we had spent many years working in corporate America, and each of us had sat through *lots* of bad meetings. One bad meeting wasn't the end of the world. And Carol was one of the people most excited and engaged in our new set of activities. What was going on here? And what would happen if Carol did leave? There were a bunch of questions we hadn't dealt with yet as a group: What *would* happen when people left, as they were bound to at some point? Could new people be incorporated into the group? If so, how would we decide who they should be? And how would we deal with serious disagreements, or the dreaded yet ever possible "personality conflicts"? We hadn't yet faced any of these questions.

Carol's email had been sent at 11:44 PM and I had picked it up after midnight. It was too late to call, but I sent back some email, and called Judy the next morning. I thought Judy would be the best person to talk to Carol and find out what was going on, since she and Carol had been working together on a Bestseller chapter. Judy was headed to Santa Fe that day and I wanted to make sure she talked to Carol before she left.

Over the next couple of days, phone calls and emails flew back and forth. Trying to find out what was happening was a bit of a Roshomon exercise. Each of us had our own interpretation and our own reaction. Judy was furious that the agenda and the ensuing discussion had allowed no time for discussing the work that she and Carol had done. And angrier still that we were discussing something that she thought was different from what was supposed to be done. Dana was worried that all the work we were doing was going to go for naught unless we could "explain it to someone in an elevator." Pam and I hadn't been to the previous meeting, and sat through this one trying to figure out what was going on. Pam sat quietly, watching people cut each other off, unable to get a word in edgewise.

I, unfortunately, had gotten caught up in the discussion of the "big questions" and missed yet another opportunity to keep my mouth shut. Yvonne was annoyed that none of us had tried to change the agenda if we thought it was wrong. After all, she'd reviewed it before we started the meeting. She thought everybody was overreacting. And what about Carol? Carol, it turned out, had been frustrated not that we weren't covering her stuff or Judy's, but that we weren't covering any new ground and were just rehashing unresolved issues.

Everybody had been unhappy about how the meeting had gone, for many different reasons, almost none of these expressed. Some of us had tried – ineffectively – to get it straightened out. Some of us had zoned out. It was a real train wreck. A management consultant would have had a field day. There were enough lessons here for several books on group dynamics. It was too bad we hadn't made a video.

On the other hand, now that Carol had sent this email, we all went into action. Everyone wanted Carol to stay part of the group. By the next day, Carol was staying – at least tentatively – and we were all trying to figure out what went wrong and how to fix it. Some of us were quick to assume responsibility and blame, others to take offense, others to try to smooth things over. It was clear that Carol's reaction was only the catalyst, and if Carol hadn't reacted someone else would have. Everybody was, all of a sudden, much more sensitive. I was really nervous about the next meeting.

Yvonne, who had facilitated most of the previous meetings, asked Carol if she would lead this one. This was a good decision because it allowed Carol to shape the meeting, and took Yvonne off the hook a little. We did our standard "check-in" to find out what everybody had been up to for the last couple of weeks, then Carol proposed we each talk about where we thought the group was heading and what we each thought about it. This gave us each a chance to talk about our own differing views of where we are and what we should and shouldn't be doing and our concerns about our individual roles in the process.

The meeting was a more sober and serious meeting than most of our previous meetings had been, but upbeat nonetheless. It clarified what we agreed on and what we disagreed on with regard to our next steps and future business direction. We had previously talked about style differences, but spent more time talking about these and their impact. My risk-averse style, for example, is three sigma from Yvonne's belief that the talents in the group should enable us to "do something *big*." Dana's desire to work within the group runs counter to Judy's to go off on her own and come back with a polished product. We all recognize intellectually that each of these styles has something to contribute, but the reality of dealing with the differences is something we still have to work through. We took steps to identify what went wrong and we decided to do some things differently: have different people in the leadership role; clearly write down and annunciate decisions; try to identify and resolve issues early, or consciously put them in a "parking lot" to be addressed later. We recognized that we will continue to make mistakes and, at the same time, we will work to not make the *same* mistakes. But mostly our discussions reaffirmed how much this group has come to mean to us and how much we enjoy it and want to succeed. And because of the trust and respect we all now have for each other, we were pretty confident we could work through this "crisis."

And we have. *The meeting*, which is the way we now laughingly refer to it, occurred in early April. It is now five months later. Carol is back in the fold – she never left – and we are all hard at work at trying to write these essays and put together a book. Working together on something concrete, out of our normal comfort zone, with the realities of conflicts and deadlines and each of our different styles, periodically stresses our normal camaraderie and our considerable skills in dealing with our differences. We periodically schedule refresh days – our last, an overnight at Kathy's house on Long Beach Island – to make sure we still know we are having fun and recognize the importance of the relationships we've created. We are out of the giddy, high, "discovery" stage that – amazingly – lasted over a year. We are onto the next stage, working together and learning to deal with our different styles and personalities and views, because the rewards in terms of our personal growth, the relationships we've created and the intellectual satisfaction of working on something together are so much greater than the individual efforts we put in.

As I see it, there are analogies between what happens in the group and my own experiences as a would-be artist and designer. I love the drawing and painting I'm doing, but there are times when I am truly frustrated and discouraged; when it seems like I will never effectively put pencil or brush to paper or do another design I like. At those times I survey whatever good work is sitting in my files and think it was a lucky accident that I won't be able to repeat. Sometimes I can regain my perspective when I review my paintings of a flower that isn't available year-round – like the bearded irises that Ed grows that bloom every June – and see the differences between what I can do this year and what I did last year. I still don't have the confidence that I can *really* do this, but I can see that I am getting better. Sometimes even that doesn't work and I know I just need to keep on plowing through this temporary abyss until I come out the other side.

The dynamics in our group are like that. Most of the time we are operating like a well-oiled engine – what, in my management training classes we used to call a "high performance team" – and then there are the occasional times when we think we all should be committed. The latter are discouraging and always temporarily take the wind out of our sails, but as with my painting, when I look back at where we are now and what we have done, I know we are doing something good, and that we are growing, each of us individually, and all of us as a group.

The satisfaction is just incredible.

Hanging Out With Older People

Pam Hufnagel

"If you want to keep looking young, hang out with older people."
- Milton Berle

I'm the youngest member of *NineWomen* and at the tail end of the baby boomer generation. Frankly, when Yvonne first asked me to join this group in late 2001, I thought it would be a great thing to do while I was in the rank and file of the unemployed. I only knew Yvonne and Carol and didn't have any preconceived notions about what we were going to accomplish. Less than six months prior to Yvonne's suggestion of forming a group, I elected to take a generous severance package from AT&T Broadband, where I was VP of Market Development and Operations. I had been in the corporate world for eighteen years and thought I needed some time off to reenergize from the constant travel and the intense seventy-hour work weeks. For the last six months of my job, my husband and I would try and arrange our Monday morning limo rides to the airport together – with me on my way to Denver and he to Washington DC where we both had executive apartments that we called each other from during the work week.

Planning to go back to work soon, I'd already started my job search, but the idea of the group appealed to me. It would be a good diversion from the job hunt. I could use my intellect instead of just riding a roller-coaster through the emotional ups and downs of interviews and rejections. One and one half years later, I was surprised to find myself still sitting on the sidelines of the employment market. This group of nine is much more than a diversion now – it's something I look forward to; it's the female mentors I wished I had during my career; it is proof that there is life after retirement. The group meetings provide a constant flow of new ideas, books to read, places to go, and ideas to think about. Continual growth has always been very important to me, both professionally and personally.

"Feminism is not a doctrine that seeks to confine us but rather a quest we continually define."

- Caroline Soriosis

During a number of meetings, the topic of feminism came up, and one day we went around the room, each answering the question: Are you a feminist?

"I never considered myself a feminist," I said. The word 'feminist' seemed too radical with a negative edge. In my mind, I pictured feminists as wild women screaming in the streets, burning bras and attacking the male chauvinists, but I was too young during that time in the 60's and 70's to live and experience what it was like to be a woman in and outside of the workplace like the other eight women did.

I'm strongly in favor of women being individuals and having an equal place in the workplace and society. I was naïve early in my career. I felt you could get ahead solely because of your abilities. Later, I realized there was an inner circle, and at times, I felt like the outsider.

Many of the others in the group participated in the women's movement of the 1960's and 1970's both actively, by attending feminist movement events, and more subtly, by going to college, majoring in male-dominated fields such as mathematics or engineering, holding off on marriage, and entering the male-dominated corporate world. Kathy told me she didn't protest through the symbolic bra burning events, because she rarely wore one in those days! Yvonne's focus was "equal pay and equality of access to opportunities for all," which she promoted by establishing a group at Bell Labs that supported women in making them stronger as individuals and as a group.

There are twenty years between the oldest member, Judy, and me. There were a lot of things that were different in each of our careers. Surprisingly, there were also a lot of similarities. Judy's story of how she chose a college and an engineering major was incredibly foreign to me.

Judy's mother was a valedictorian of her high school and went to one year of college, but wasn't allowed to return after her mom got mad at her because she went to a dance with a boy. Because of that old hurt, Judy's mother made sure that by the first grade her daughter was already working to get into college. By the end of high school, Judy had her heart set on going to Chatham College in Pittsburgh to become a writer. She was devastated when she learned that they would not give her a scholarship, as they didn't believe her father would be able to pay the room and board that was required, since he was already helping to support her older brother's education. Upset that her dream was being dismantled, she marched over to Carnegie Mellon University, where she'd also applied, and asked to see the Dean immediately. She and the Dean made a deal. If Judy would enter his newly designed program in technical writing, he'd get her a scholarship that included room and board. When she had to choose a focus for her technical writing, she didn't know what she should pick among the offerings – mathematics, chemistry or biology. She asked her older brother, who was at the same college working on his Ph.D. His response changed her life.

"Be different," he said. "Tell them you want to focus on electrical engineering. That should give the administration something to think about."

After hearing Judy's story, I felt like I better understood what women before me had done in order to open doors that were once closed. A lot had occurred to unlock those big, heavy doors in twenty years.

When I was ready to apply for college twenty years later in the late 1970's, the educational landscape had completely altered and opened up opportunities for women that had been difficult, if not impossible, before. It never occurred to me that I wouldn't attend college and I felt no pressures about where I should go or what I should pursue.

I felt I lived my mother's dreams of having a choice. When she attended college, she had three professions that she could choose from – teaching, becoming a secretary, and nursing. I had many choices and felt the whole world was waiting for me with open arms when I was ready for college. I had always wanted to work in the business world. In fact, when I was in first grade, we were asked what we wanted to be when we grew up. Some said President of the United States; others mentioned teaching or being a mother. I very clearly told the teacher I was going to sell shoes! Unlike my mother, I felt there were no overt barriers. I pursued a marketing major at Georgetown University's business school. (By the way, I still love shoes.)

Yvonne, who is in her mid 50's, told the group about how her mother instilled the value of education and career in her. Yvonne's mother had left Puerto Rico to attend college in the U.S., and had always planned that Yvonne and her sister would also attend college in the states. "She had a very significant influence on us and was a strong-willed business woman." Yvonne said, "so she took a wise approach when I told her I didn't want to go to college, and instead wanted to be a beautician." Her mother responded, "Do you want to run a beauty parlor, or do you want to be the beautician who works there?" "I want to run the place," Yvonne answered. "Then go to college," her mother said. So she did.

Many of us had strong mothers who helped to form our values and priorities. In my case, as well as Margaret Ann's, the male role model heavily influenced us in our pursuit of education. My grandfather was a driving force behind my appreciation for academic success. I grew up listening to him tell stories from his childhood and describe his aspirations for his family to have more opportunities than he did. As his stories unfurled, the smoke from his pipe would swirl around like a cloud around our heads. He'd been the youngest in a German immigrant family of nine where a strong work ethic was the pervasive theme. Even though his older brothers were allowed to go to college, it was never an option for him. His father demanded that he do handiwork in the many rental homes that they owned. Never bitter, he placed a very high priority on education, and the value of education was passed down through my mother to my sister and me. It may not have been the same story, but I heard about the value of education from many of the others in our group.

Margaret Ann was from a family of four children in which she was the only girl. Her father, from a working-class family, got a scholarship and worked his way through college. He was adamant that all four of his children would attend college and get graduate degrees. Margaret Ann told the group about the only argument she ever had with her father.

"I told him I wasn't going to graduate school. He told me if I didn't go to graduate school, I'd only be able to drive a garbage truck. He was so mad; he hung up the phone on me. I cried, but I have two postgraduate degrees."

My parents both had graduate degrees. I knew that they would pay for college, but I would be responsible for financing my graduate degree if I decided to pursue one. I worked for a number of years before pursuing an MBA at Seton Hall University. I was very fortunate at that time, my education was one hundred percent covered under AT&T's benefits. My primary reason for pursuing an MBA was to help me in my career. I knew that while studying for an MBA at night and on weekends coupled with a demanding job, I would not be able to spend as much time learning, but would need to have a "just get through it" mentality. But I felt it was important to help set me apart. At that time, college degrees were becoming the standard for both men and women in the corporate world. For me, receiving an MBA was checking off one more box.

"But the problem is that when I go around and speak on campuses, I still don't get young men standing up and saying, 'How can I combine career and family?'"

- Gertrude Stein

All the women in the group had been encouraged to have a career. But usually career was sold as a good fallback position, if we needed money or if (God forbid!) a husband died. In my case, marriage was not emphasized; in fact, it was de-emphasized. My mother got married during her senior year of college, had my sister one year later, and me 18 months later. She and my dad struggled to make ends meet while establishing their careers, furthering their education with MBAs and raising two toddlers while trying to build a marriage. Despite having an MBA, a good job, two children and a marriage that was strong, my mother's indirect message to me was that marriage ties you down and holds you back, while a career provides freedom and independence. I knew from how she encouraged me that she would have liked to run a company like her dad did or become a professional in the corporate world. She is a very smart and assertive woman and I think she felt unfulfilled in being forced to pursue a career in teaching math to seventh graders.

As a result, I didn't think I ever wanted to get married. I was definitely in no hurry, wanting to focus instead on my career. By the time I did get married in my late 30's, I had established myself professionally, filled my wanderlust living and traveling extensively in Europe, and received my MBA. The one thing that was missing was having children. That is one of my only regrets. I was so focused on my goal of becoming successful in my career that I didn't spend the time and effort needed to develop a relationship. I foolishly hoped that would just occur naturally. Then I realized: How could that happen when I was spending most of my waking hours at work or school?

Amazingly, during the 60+ hour weeks when I was working and finishing my MBA, I met my future husband on the job. It took us six years to get married, which at times, seemed like an eternity. He has two children from a prior marriage, is older than I, and not at all interested in having children again. He was commitment-shy, and fearful of making a mistake after having gone through a divorce. I, on the other hand, knew he was the right man for me, wanted to get married after a year of dating, and was hoping he might change his mind about having children. Now, you can understand why it took us six years to get married! There were some painful discussions and a raw emptiness at times, knowing I would never have children with him. I think I would have been a great mother and envy those women I see who can do it all, but I wasn't fortunate enough – or maybe just didn't have the foresight – to follow that path in life.

After leaving my job, which happened to coincide with the terrible and devastating terrorist attacks of September 11, 2001, I brought my husband to a standard poodle breeder and we adopted a beautiful, brown eight-week-old puppy, which we named Bailey. Certainly he can't take the place of having children, but he has been a true joy and causes me to laugh every day. The emptiness I feel when alone on a rainy day with time to think about what might have been in my life with children, is soothed when I peer into Bailey's big brown adoring eyes or hug his soft curly-haired body next to mine. Deep down, I know he helps to fill that void, but I don't like to think about that very much.

"The only jobs for which no man is qualified are human incubator and wet nurse. Likewise, the only job for which no women is or can be qualified is sperm donor."

-       *Wilma Scott Heide*

I listened with surprise to the stories others told about the difficulties of their first promotion. Fran told about the day in 1971 when she was first asked to be a supervisor. She knew at the time about what had happened when Judy had been promoted. One man out of a group of five had told Judy's boss that two of the other men were going to quit because Judy was being promoted to supervisor. Her boss handled it competently and they'd stayed, but it had been a tough ordeal. Fran wasn't sure she wanted to endure an experience like that. She wasn't sure she ever wanted to be a manager; and she was concerned she wasn't that knowledgeable in this particular area of systems development. Needing guidance, she called Judy to discuss the situation. The funny part of the story was that Judy was home on maternity leave and happened to have already gone into labor when Fran called. But because Judy appreciated the diversion from her pain, she didn't tell Fran about her contractions during the half-hour her husband was driving home from work to take her to the hospital. By the time Judy's husband arrived, they'd decided that Fran should not accept that particular job, but should make it clear she'd be interested in another offer. Within three months, Fran was made a Bell Labs supervisor, which meant she would now have people working for her. At that time, she was one of eight female technical managers in all of Bell Labs.

The climate for women was very different when I was first promoted at AT&T in 1990. Before even starting there at 28, I had worked for four different companies and had lived and worked in Germany. When I returned from Germany, I was interviewing with a number of large companies including AT&T, IBM, and Xerox. I decided I needed to settle down in one location, and would benefit from working for a large corporation because I could move around from department to department, easing my fears of boredom while learning and growing. I was hired into an entry-level manager position and decided after about three months that I was qualified for promotion. I already had visions of being in my boss's position managing a group of fifty people.

Unlike Fran, there was no fear there, although I could have been more realistic. I did get promoted within two years into an international marketing position. The leader of the whole organization was a female and my boss's boss was also a woman. Certainly, I was very fortunate to have a number of females in leadership positions above me. Unlike the situation at the time for Judy, Fran and others from our group, the path had already been created, which in some ways made it easier for me. In other ways, it created an expectation of what success meant.

Fran, when talking about her first promotion, observed that, in her experience, men would take any job that was offered to them, assuming they would be able to figure it out later, whereas women were much more concerned about whether they had the specific skills and actually could DO the job. Even though women were in executive positions "showing me the way," as my career progressed, I felt the same way Fran had years earlier. "Can I really DO the job?" I didn't take enough advantage of asking senior executives to help coach me or mentor me. I thought that if I excelled at my job, it would show what I could do, so I just tried to work harder and better. However, the successful men in my peer group were more likely to develop strong relationships in addition to focusing on their jobs to move their careers forward more quickly.

Our group developed the phrase "mommy's good girl" syndrome to describe our tendency to just try and do a better job when the going got tough instead of attempting to "wheel and deal," make waves, or take advantage of relationships like the men did. I was exhibiting the same behavior I did growing up. I was a good girl if I put my head down and focused, or quietly completed all of my chores, got good grades and didn't get into trouble!

"I base most of my fashion sense on what doesn't itch."

- Gilda Radner

Dressing for the role was also a part of the package and most of our group told stories about choosing clothes that would ensure we fit in. Carol read the book *Dress for Success* by John T. Molloy and became an immediate follower by buying twenty-one suits, high-necked blouses and sensible but boring shoes. Dana took a different approach, cleverly selecting her clothes to stand out in the way she wanted to be viewed that day.

Dressing appropriately was also a way of defining myself in the corporate world. The leather skirts and patterned stockings that I wore while living in Europe in my 20's were put away, replaced by conservative blue, black and taupe outfits, plain silk blouses with black patent leather shoes in my 30's. For me, in a sense, dressing the part, toned down my personality, and was one of the walls I put up to keep my personal and business life separate. Even now with dress down or a business casual dress policy, the uniform that many women wear is chinos or khakis, which is what the men wear. It's strange – twenty-five years ago, women adopted male-style ties, then we moved to pin stripe pants suits – now we are wearing khakis! Even after many years of women working in corporate America, it still appears as though women are trying to assimilate into the corporate male mold versus wearing their individual femininity with pride.

"The great thing in this world is not where we are, but in what direction we are moving."

– Oliver Wendell Holmes

This has been an incredible journey. All of us are moving forward individually and collectively. For me, it's back to the corporation to unleash that "big bang" that I've still got inside of me. During the writing of this, I received a job offer from AT&T Wireless thrusting me back into the corporate working world. I'm proud and happy because it's still tough finding a good job in the telecommunications industry. I'm also pleased to be returning armed with more than industry knowledge and professional skills – I've got eight dynamic female mentors in my cheering section who have taught me to appreciate and accept that "success" is what you create, not what is prescribed or expected.

This intimate group has helped me to come to this realization, and it's my plan to continue my journey with them even though I won't be able to go to the regular meetings. I intend to help define a new kind of membership. A little envious of the older group members, I also look joyously forward to the time when I can fully embrace that next stage in my life when I will feed my passions and nurture my creativity in new ways. You can be assured that each Act II, and maybe in some cases Act III, will not be the expected. Stay tuned – there's much more to come. Being the youngest of the group, I know that now.

I Am My Father's Daughter

Margaret Ann Chappell

My boss called me while I was on a business trip in June, 2001, and told me Lucent was offering early retirement. What a curious way to start a day! I'd just turned 50. I was certainly too young to retire. But the telecom industry was in a slump and life at work had become truly miserable – the perpetual downsizing and finger pointing was becoming an unacceptable way of life. I realized that perhaps I'd been given a golden opportunity. I could take the summer off – giving me time to cultivate my rose garden and to travel. In September, I could figure out what to do next.

After much internal debate, I retired, feeling that life had so much more to offer and I had more to give to it. It was time to move on. Scary. But usually change is scary. In the past, I'd always known what I'd do next – get into college, go to graduate school, get a job. This juncture was different. I had no roadmap. Or role model.

Though that phone call from my boss occurred only two years ago, the world and I have changed significantly since then. I spent the summer of 2001 as I'd hoped – cleaning up years of clutter, cultivating a wonderful garden, traveling, discovering distant relatives, lunching with friends – activities that were delightful but did not really address what I should do when I grow up. I still haven't formulated a plan. But I've become more accepting of the uncertainty and confident of the future. At first, I didn't tell anyone that I'd retired. Rather, I was on sabbatical.

I had lunch with Yvonne and a mutual friend who was visiting from out of town in late September, 2001. We were still reeling from September 11th. I was struggling with "retirement." I kept asking them about their transition into retirement. We all wanted to do something meaningful, but didn't quite know what. It was clear from our discussion that there was no obvious answer. It was also clear that we collectively knew a lot of talented women who were struggling with the same issues – struggling to find something meaningful after leaving the corporate world while at the same time being able to maintain a sense of balance in their lives. September 11th had given us a sense of urgency. Yvonne called me later that day with the idea of getting a group of women together to explore how we collectively might tackle some of the ideas we had discussed at lunch. The Brain Trust was beginning. I was excited.

A few months later we were ready to have our first meeting. When Yvonne told me who would be gathering, I almost didn't go. Everyone was much more "successful" than I was. There were former corporate officers and executives and entrepreneurs – and me. I was definitely intimidated. I was a technologist, not an executive – and the business world that I'd come from certainly valued its executives more than its technologists. On the first day, as the women started talking about themselves, I relaxed. Everyone's humanness transcended their old-world titles and positions. As we explored what activities or business we wanted to do as a group, we discovered that we shared common values.

Many of us had become involved in fitness programs. Our priorities had shifted, as well as our bodies. We had to work to get ourselves in shape. Overall health was important if we were to succeed in our future endeavors. Discussions of menopause frequently crept into our conversations. When the Women's Health Initiative Study prematurely halted its HRT component and the popular press was abuzz with hormone replacement therapy stories we realized that we, like most women, were confused by all the conflicting medical studies. We started sharing articles. Some of us joined legions of women in getting off hormones. We had to have the thermostat in our conference room adjusted multiple times per meeting as one of us started to melt down.

Fire Island really helped to solidify our group. Most of us only knew Duffy as a voice. She'd primarily joined the group via conference call from Florida. We all looked forward to getting to know her. As we raced across Long Island Sound in a water taxi with the wind flying through our hair and the salt spraying in our faces, you could feel the energy and excitement building. It was hard to believe – eight retired women on our way to a sleepover! The energy and excitement remained long after we'd returned from Dana's house on the barrier island.

In Yvonne's car on the way home we started talking about possible future activities and Fran mentioned the "Drawing on the Right Side of the Brain" class. Yvonne and I declared that we were artistically challenged. The thought of exploring drawing with a supportive group was intriguing.

There could not have been a more perfect environment for exploring an area in which I "knew" I had no talent. I was absolutely stunned by some of my drawings. My body must have been invaded by aliens when I drew my hand for the third time. It actually looked like my hand. And I had drawn it! Then there was my chair. My chair drawing seemed to provide the best entertainment during our class. I dutifully measured the arms and legs like a good scientist. I guess I'd temporarily forgotten to use the *right* side of my brain. My left brain produced a wonderfully lopsided, unstable chair!

After the drawing class I realized that I probably could draw if I spent the time and energy to learn the techniques. And if I was given the spirited encouragement I received from my friends and our instructor. Since I was a kid,

I'd thought I had no artistic talent. In reality, I'd never really tried to learn how to draw. I began wondering if my old beliefs created other things I "knew" I couldn't do, limiting my willingness to challenge myself. It didn't take long to find other examples.

My old-time phobia about anything athletic surfaced again. I had always "flunked" gym. With trepidation I had joined a health club. In my initial strength assessment I didn't even make it onto the bottom of the charts that plotted women's strength. I knew I had to do something since women lose muscle mass as they age and I had none to lose. I wasn't sure what would happen as I lost my miniscule amount of muscle, but knew I didn't want to find out. Oddly, it was the drawing class that gave me the tenacity I needed. If I could draw given the right encouragement, I could get stronger given the right training. After about a year of serious commitment, I'm in the 70th percentile on that strength chart!

Between Fire Island and the drawing class we had been answering our questionnaire. I found it fascinating. First, as I worked through answering the questions, patterns in my life began to emerge. I discovered how surprisingly consistent in my values I'd been as I progressed through the stages of my life. Family, life-long learning, and the independence that enabled me to take care of myself were always critical for me. I'd never consciously thought about it before.

Then, I was amazed by the patterns within the group which surfaced when we shared our answers. Our mothers were strong. Education was essential. We weren't good career planners. Independence was highly valued, particularly financial independence. Each of us frequently felt like an outsider or imposter. Any residual feeling I had of being different, because I hadn't chosen the management path, evaporated as we talked and laughed our way through the questionnaire.

I enjoyed the human qualities of each group member. Pam recollected how though her family participated in a wide range of activities, they always managed to be home for dinner together. Yvonne, who'd grown up in Puerto Rico, described her first encounter with snow while she was in college – it wasn't creamy like she'd thought and it was so quiet. Fran's father didn't want her to end up like her spinster aunt. Kathy's mother had once warned her future husband to be wary of her daughter; he'd likely as not be dumped. Judy's dad wanted her to get married, have children, and avoid being the cranky teacher his sister had become. Dana told how her mother encouraged her not to fear all the moves her family made because of her father's job. "Take advantage of the change," her mother said. "You get to decide who you want to be in the new town."

Sometimes a story would hit a group nerve. Duffy told a story of how she was so caught up with work – terribly busy yet very organized and methodical. One day her sister called and wanted to see her. Duffy told her secretary to make an appointment for her sister. That evening Duffy was totally distraught as she'd realized how messed up her priorities had become. How could she possibly ask her sister to make an appointment to see her? Her pain and embarrassment came through when she told this story all these years later. Duffy's story unleashed a torrent of stories and feelings. How often had all our family priorities been usurped by our involvement in work? The guilt. The torment. The opportunities lost. They all flooded back.

The outpouring of emotions and stories was enlightening to me. Frequently I'd been the family member who had plans ruined because my executive husband had to cancel trips due to a work crisis. I could only recall one or two times in my career when I had to renege on personal commitments because of work. As we talked, I was thinking how lucky I'd been to have the freedom that I strove for at work. The example that immediately came to mind starkly contrasted my personal flexibility with the demands placed on executives. When my father was terminally ill and in intensive care for months, I was able to repeatedly fly to his side to be with him and my mother. I could never have taken the time to spend with them during this time had I been an executive. In fact, the time I was most angry with the intrusiveness of the corporation, was when my husband's company insisted that he participate on a conference call while he was at the funeral home helping to make my father's funeral arrangements. A perfect example of how out-of-balance and out-of-touch executive corporate life had become. Discussing priorities that day helped me better appreciate how appropriate my career choices had been for me.

Sometimes the group's reaction to a story was surprising – at least to the storyteller. I told about how education was my father's overriding goal for all of his children. I have three brothers and my father expected all of us to excel in school. He was far ahead of the time by expecting his only daughter to perform to the same standards as his sons, to get an advanced degree, and to go on to a career. He set the standards by his performance. Every marking period, when our report cards arrived, my father sat down with each of us individually and compared our grades to his. He pulled out report cards that he'd saved from grammar school through college and searched for the comparable one. I think he might have had a B somewhere in high school. The standard was clear.

I thought I was just telling the group a story from my past. Well, the group became hysterical. People laughed and gasped in disbelief. "Are you making this up?" they asked. "Have you saved *your* report cards?" No one else's father had set this kind of standard. I'd never thought twice about it. Suddenly I understood the impetus behind my perfectionism and high personal standards. The group's reaction reinforced something I'd known, but had never before articulated so clearly – that my father was truly a visionary in his opinion of the life he believed his daughter should lead.

Early on in this essay, I said I'd changed over the past two years. Our group has been an important part of the change. Doors to new experiences have been opened. Past doubts and questions have become unimportant. This transition – into my next life phase and beyond –

with a group of intelligent, fun, and supportive women, has helped make what could very easily have been a scary and depressing transition into a broader, more creative experience.

I've started taking photography classes. I've always loved photography and have fond memories of taking pictures with my dad as a child and developing them in his darkroom. I'd say that I never had the time to pursue photography, but more likely it was my belief that I lacked artistic talent that held me back. Now I'm engrossed in photography and enjoying the melding of the art of photography with the emerging tools of the digital darkroom. I'm using my computer skills in a new and much more creative way. Do I know where my venture into photography will lead? Not really. Will I become a professional photographer? Who knows? For once in my life, I'm pursuing a passion with no clear end goals and it's amazingly fun!

For me, an important element of the experiences we've been sharing is gaining perspective. In the corporate environment it was easy to get caught up into what the corporation and culture defined as success – how fast and how far you moved up the corporate ladder. I early on decided that wasn't the path for me. So while I always excelled at what I did, I never really felt like I was successful. It didn't matter that I had a Ph.D., could get virtually any technical job I wanted, or had a wonderful salary. There was always that nagging sense that I somehow wasn't successful. I was never quite comfortable with my decision to stay technical or the consequences of it.

After listening to everyone's stories, reflecting on my own story, and interacting with the group in our informal meandering way – I no longer have the same view of success or vague feeling about being unsuccessful. The path I chose was consistent with my personal values. It was the right one for me. I (usually) don't think of myself as less successful than the rest of the group anymore. They, not infrequently, playfully remind me that the standards I set for myself are a little high. I guess I learned my father's lessons well. Thanks Dad!

A Diagnosis

Dana Becker Dunn

I was ready to leave the corporate world. It was August 1, 2001. I was 50. I felt I had lost my ability to maintain a good balance between work, family, and personal interests during the last ten years of my 29-year career; a career that started at Bell Labs and moved through the AT&T divestiture, two company spin-offs (Lucent and Avaya), and a significant involvement in the changing role of women in these companies. I longed for more time to pursue my other interests and to be with my husband, Brian, my eleven-year-old son, Patrick, and my step daughter,

114

Kerry, and her growing family. Renewing and extending friendships was also very important to me, but I had no preconceived ideas about how I'd do that.

Early in the summer of 2001, Avaya announced that they would be changing the retirement age from 50 to 55 on August 1, 2001. My plan had always been to retire at the young age of 50, so I did. The first priority of my retirement was to get back into good physical shape, something that had been ignored for many years. I began to work out with a personal trainer three mornings a week and do some kind of aerobic exercise three to four times a week. I tackled my eating habits as well.

Then I began to pursue a long list of new and challenging interests left dormant for most of my adult life. I immersed myself in several art courses focused on different media – oil, pastel, watercolor, stained glass, and digital photography. I joined the Garden Club in town and began to spend more time encouraging and enjoying my own flower gardens. I renewed a long-time love of mine, cooking, by taking several short courses and updating my seriously out-of-date recipe database. Several of my friends knit, needlepoint, and quilt. You guessed it: I also began to experiment with needlework again, something I had learned as a child from my mother.

It was so wonderful to be on such a steep learning curve again. Every session I attended was filled with new "ah ha's." Some friends and I formed an impromptu painting and knitting group. We gathered at the studio apartment over my garage once a week, and even though we were all beginners, we helped each other practice our new found interests.

My son Patrick and I enjoyed breakfast and the occasional late afternoon together affording me a stronger sense of his character and humor. This past Mother's Day he gave me a great card that reflects his sense of humor. The front, "Hey Mom! Thanks for teaching me so many wonderful things over the years." And as you turn the page it reads, "Especially that potty training thing! (I can't tell you how many times that has come in handy.) Happy Mother's Day." It is wonderful to be available and share the experiences of everyday life with him as he continues to grow. And, likewise, it is terrific to spend quality time with Kerry and my grandchildren, Innes (4 years), and Finlay (1 ½ years).

As a family, we went on some great vacations. We cruised the Mediterranean from Istanbul, Turkey to Barcelona, Spain. We explored the Southern Hemisphere in Australia, New Zealand, Tasmania, and back through Hawaii. We toured around Northern Ireland. We love to travel and have many more parts of the world left to see.

I kept connected with "corporate America" by maintaining my board-of-directors position with a financial services company. It was just enough to keep me in touch with current market conditions, new business experiences, and past business associates.

So, as you can see, I didn't need something else to do; I didn't miss my "work schedule." I did not even have time to do the things I was passionate about.

Then along came Yvonne, asking me to join a group of women and to form the group we now call *NineWomen*. It interested me as another learning experience and an intellectual challenge, but quite frankly, I joined because Yvonne asked me.

It has been a fascinating journey as the group has shared past life stories and current experiences. I have thoroughly enjoyed the learning adventures from trekking the beach at Fire Island, "Drawing on the Right side of the Brain," exploring Duke Gardens in all its splendor during our dreary winter, eating at the Thai restaurant (a food style I thought I didn't like, until this experience), to trying to understand the New Jersey Government (still somewhat a mystery). These things all fit right into my interest in exploring new areas. As we moved into the second year of working together, I had such a sense of well-being and connectedness with this group and a genuine feeling of friendship with each of the individuals, most of whom I did not know well before we began.

So what happened? How did we get to this point? What made the difference in this group formation? Why am I still engaged?

I believe that the time we spent creating the questionnaire and sharing our life stories by way of the questionnaire galvanized the group. Creating the questionnaire allowed us to determine what areas of our history were important in meeting our personal goals and in formulating our approach to helping other women in transition. We also wanted to span the generations and help younger women succeed. We thought that other groups might use our questionnaire, but realized that a group with different backgrounds and ages might develop a significantly different questionnaire. It also seemed possible that for other groups, creating the questionnaire might play an important role in the development of the group itself.

After each of us filled out the questionnaire independently, we went around the table and each person answered the same one or two questions. Although, as Kathy mentioned, it took over six months, I think this process was important from several vantage points. First, it gave each person adequate time to share important information about her history and life. After all, we were each accomplished women used to having some form of audience for our thoughts and ideas. Second, it allowed everyone to focus on the speaker and really listen to her stories and experiences. In other words, we knew that we would have the opportunity to share our stories later, so it encouraged us to listen to the others. Finally, this helped to create an open, sharing environment, which I believe was critical to deepening the groups' relationships and connectedness. We gained insights about ourselves and each other. Events that we had assumed only happened to us as individuals turned out to be common experiences. It wasn't just that most of us had once felt like outsiders.

Even though we realized that others would consider all of us to be in very good shape with regard to money, financial security was still critical to each of us because we needed to retain the independence we'd worked so hard to achieve. Despite our successes, most of us still had trouble expressing the harsh reality of our having enjoyed business power and the ethical dilemmas that we had to face and resolve as business leaders.

Although Yvonne did bring us together originally, we used a self-directed approach to decide on agendas, next steps, and even new adventures. The process of the group evolved in an organic way as the member relationships matured. Following our instincts rather than structure has been an important element in my staying interested and engaged in the group. I spent so many years focused on goals, deadlines, and due dates that I needed some time and space to participate and generate without feeling pressured; to explore ideas even if they did not lead to an important milestone. This open-ended process served as a strong foundation for the entire group to be creative and to accept ownership for the progress we have made, and was another important ingredient in the recipe for success.

For me, it is also important to recall the more difficult aspect of our group relationship: differences in the working styles. I, for one, along with Yvonne, Duffy, Fran and Pam prefer to interact with others when generating ideas and plans for the group. The other half prefer to take time to ponder the question quietly on their own time, record their thoughts, and then bring these back to the group for a more generative conversation. Interestingly, the questionnaire accommodated both of these styles quite well. But as we began tackling projects, it was frustrating for me at times to be on the brink of a great creative conversation and have someone say, "Let's take that offline and talk about it next time. Why don't we write down our ideas and e-mail them to everyone?" Somehow it left me feeling empty. Frustrated that I was supposed to go home, stare at an empty page and do more work alone, I wondered, *If that's the case, why am I even part of a group? Why should I have to work alone?* I sometimes just waited until the next meeting to be creative. But then, of course, I felt guilty because I hadn't done my homework.

Some of us preferred to tackle a problem top down, from the "big picture perspective." Others wanted to go ahead and pick a project, work on it, and answer the larger questions later, but get something done in the meantime. As we proceeded to work on the details of the pamphlet project (this book started out as a pamphlet), I was agitated that we had not answered some key questions. I felt that we might waste time on an activity and then have to go back and redo our work. As I reflect on this reaction, I recognize that we didn't have a deadline and that it does feel good sometimes to move the ball forward by completing some activities.

I believe that these key differences in style led to the crescendo of the disagreements at that meeting Fran mentioned. And yet each of our styles created a successful career and I suspect this diversity of style will lead to a more successful group as we proceed. In fact, the breakdown may make us a stronger, more related and productive group as we continue.

I am drawn to this group for many reasons: the friendships, the intellectual stimulation, the fun, the curiosity of what makes a group like this one tick, and the likelihood that we will make a contribution to others in a meaningful way. I will be going on an exciting adventure with my family next year to live in Killarney, Ireland while Patrick attends his eighth grade year abroad. I will be extremely busy. And guess what I did! As reluctant as I'd been to join the group, still sometimes frustrated by our different working styles, I asked the other women if they'd be willing to schedule some of the meetings next year on days that I will be back from Ireland for my board meetings. They have graciously agreed.

Why do I want to stay part of the group? It isn't just the wonderful friends. I make friends easily. One of my personal goals over the course of my life is to make a difference for other women as I learn and grow, to share experiences that can help others to enjoy a more full life. *NineWomen* has been a very special experience for me on my journey toward this goal and I hope we can offer this in some meaningful way to others on the brink of Act II.

Fulfilling Dreams

Kathy Meier

"People often say that this or that person has not yet found himself. But the self is not something one finds; it is something one creates."

Thomas Szasz, U.S. psychiatrist, *The Second Sin, Personal Conduct* (1973).

Thinking Back: Anxious to leave after a career of 29 years, I retired from Lucent Technologies in the summer of 2000. I had liked my job, but had learned to hate the culture, a once grand company led awry by leaders, many from acquired companies, often with immature attitudes and unethical methods. I had always loved marketing – there is nothing like the thrill of bringing a new product to market and all the hoopla connected with talking to the press, customers and media. I loved explaining to customers how new technology could positively influence their businesses. During 1998 and 1999, I had orchestrated a marketing blitz – participating in over 60 trade shows (mostly as an expert speaker on technology and industry trends), briefing the press and media on product and technological trends, and being a lead speaker at over 100 industry and customer events. I traveled to ten countries, including Hong Kong, Tokyo, Singapore, Geneva, Mexico, and Germany plus dozens of U.S. cities. I loved the adrenaline, the excitement, the challenge, and the travel. (I conveniently forgot about all the airports, the barren hotel rooms and the lonely nights.) It was one of the best years of my career.

Then, when I retired in 2000, I did not give up my career, but instead accepted a job as an officer in charge of marketing with a small firm in Texas. I didn't relocate (my husband was clear that it was not his destiny to move to Texas) so I commuted between there and Pennsylvania every week. This may sound crazy, but, in fact, I had traveled a lot in the past decade of my career, spent many years flying over 100,000 miles and accepted 70-hour workweeks as the norm. The potential financial benefits were very attractive and I used to joke about my new adventure and getting rich. But, more significantly, I wanted to prove to myself that I could be a successful executive of a small firm. Though clearly a success at AT&T and Lucent, I was always left with a lingering question – could I be a success outside the comfort of a large corporation?

Summer 2001: I was a Vice President of Marketing for a small start-up company in the suburbs of Dallas. It had been a hectic winter and spring (it always is in marketing). My team and I had organized and participated in twelve industry shows with challenging speaking engagements and live product demonstrations and orchestrated a major product announcement. I had personally done dozens of press and media interviews and we had won three prestigious "best product of the year" awards, including one at Supercomm, a major telecommunications trade show.

I was on a high. Then reality set in. The economy was in a tail-spin; our prospective customers all seemed to be filing for Chapter 11; our Board of Directors was pressuring my boss to conserve cash and strongly suggesting that we cut the size of our company in half. My business life seemed to be scripted from a soap opera – my boss was not responding well to the pressure of being a CEO, his behavior was becoming more and more bizarre, and he had only a few friends in the company and none within the officer ranks. The founder of the company was a brilliant guy although a bit of a geek; he was also the brains behind the company and a friend of mine. Behind the scenes he was lobbying with the Chairman of the Board for a major change. This was cloak and dagger stuff. A show down was brewing; I expected a blow-up at the Board Meeting planned for September 8.

I was very thankful for a scheduled week of vacation. My husband and I had bought a house at Long Beach Island on the Jersey shore in 1984. Every year I spend a week or two at the end of August walking the beach, reading books, and reflecting on my life and career. I count on the serenity of the ocean and the beach to re-charge my spirits. Often the peace and relaxation enables me to face up to my real feelings and make tough decisions about what I want to do with my life. This year I was in for some real soul-searching.

There wasn't much peace and quiet that summer. The founder called me every day, worried that I would just give up and call it quits and not come back to Texas. My boss' emails, in preparation for the Board meeting, were threatening and incoherent; one issued an ultimatum to all the officers to reduce our departments by half and gave a target for employees being off the payroll by September 17, 2001. As I walked the beach, I realized that I was miserable. I loved my job, but the work environment was frankly not great, the politics were almost as bad as a large corporation, the commute was finally getting to me, I had no personal life, and in an "ah ha" moment I admitted that I had accomplished my goal – I was a success in this small company and had done well enough financially, although I certainly wasn't rich. On a roll from the adrenaline of brute honesty, I confessed to myself the dread of living through yet another era of downsizing. I had already lived through dozens of corporate "resizings" beginning in 1984 and those downturns were never fun. I had left Lucent to join a small company that would grow and flourish, not to repeat the depressing cycles of right-sizing that were normal in a large bureaucracy. I just couldn't do it again.

The Board meeting on September 8 was a disaster, the worst I ever had attended, but there was no blow-up, just a chilling silence from the outside Board members. This was not a good sign. I was profoundly upset. I had always had a talent for reading the tea leaves and I had a very bad feeling. I talked to my husband about the possibility of quitting. I had just received a notice that my mortgage at home was paid in full, so the financial equation was substantially improved. As usual, my husband was supportive of my decision, whatever it might be, but probed to be sure I wasn't just reacting emotionally. (I also think he was worried that if I stopped working I would be bored to tears, sitting home eating bon-bons while watching TV.)

On September 9 as I boarded American Airlines flight 2049 Newark to Dallas, I knew I had made my decision. It was time to leave. I was tired of it all – I wanted a life, a real life, I had nothing more to prove to myself in my professional life. It was time to move on; it was time to retire for real. I was giddy with anticipation and scared too. Boy would this be a big change! I was also afraid that I wouldn't be true to myself and somehow in a workaholic moment agree to stay.

On Tuesday morning September 11, I felt tired from tossing and turning all night while rehearsing how to tell my boss that I was downsizing myself. I was watching the CNBC show, Squawk Box like I did every morning. Dressed and ready to leave for work, a mere 5-minute drive, I sat on the sofa in my Texas apartment, finishing my coffee. On the TV, I noticed a close-up of the skyline of Manhattan and it looked like there was smoke in one of the buildings at the World Trade Center. I continued to watch, trying to figure out what was happening, as were the commentators on TV. As I looked at the screen, a plane flew into the second Tower and all hell broke loose. I sat on my sofa, in shock, not able to move. Finally, seeking the comfort of other people, I dragged myself to work. My meeting with my boss was set for first thing and it did not go well. I told him I was "downsizing" myself and he kept arguing with me, refusing to accept my decision. He kept suggesting other people on my staff who should be cut and I kept saying "no." I could see that he was worried about an officer leaving. I was convinced I was making the right decision and knew that my excellent staff could get the job done. Finally, I agreed to stay until December 15 to finish a strategic project that the Board had requested and to assure a smooth transition. As I left his office, I walked over to the conference room where one of the engineers had set up a television – the room was quiet and somber. As we all stood there in silence, the first Tower of the World Trade Center crumbled. I had tears in my eyes, as did every one else in the room. Then the second Tower fell and there was an audible gasp.

Eventually I went home to my apartment aware of how alone I felt. I talked to my husband on the phone, both of us making sure the other one was all right, although how could anyone really be all right? I watched television non-stop for the rest of the day. All I wanted to do was to go home and be with my husband, but I was stranded in Texas. My travel agent, who had become my friend, refused to book me on a flight home because she didn't want me to fly. I checked out Yahoo maps and discovered it would take twenty-five hours to drive home. Since September 17 was our "lay-off" day I conceded that I would stay in Dallas. It was a truly horrible week – there were only three other times in my life that I had felt that bad – when my mother died, when my brother died and when my father died. I had never felt so all alone and miserable. That Saturday I rented a couple movies to divert my attention from the unrelenting news. I was having nightmares – I kept seeing the television pictures of the World Trade Center. Talk about events putting the mundane world of business, lay-offs and careers into perspective! The phone rang and I was surprised to hear from my friend, the founder of our company. He asked if I was sitting down, and then told me that our boss had just resigned. The next day, Sunday, we had an emergency meeting of the remaining officers at my apartment – we needed to be sure we were ready for "downsizing day" and knew what to say about our boss' departure. The other officers asked me to reconsider my decision to leave, but after the last five days, I was even more convinced that my decision to leave was the right one.

I continued to commute to Texas for the next thirteen weeks. Airports and flying were pretty scary. My last official day of work was December 15.

Burned-out workaholic: Liberated after three decades of a grueling career, my first month of leisure was marked by the pleasure of days and weeks of unstructured time. I relished a new kind of freedom. I called my new existence the "no-mores": no more alarm clocks and 70-hour work weeks; no more congested highways and traffic jams; no more intrusive security screenings at airports and travel delays; no more suits and high heels and make-up and pantyhose; no more crazy bosses and ridiculous deadlines. Getting a life, I was doing what I wanted to do only when I wanted to do it. I spent hours watching junk television, reading, cooking and eating healthy meals, religiously going to the gym, organizing my finances and recipes, cleaning out the attic, and sleeping. I was euphoric.

My pleasure in being a "bum" lasted one month. Then Yvonne called and asked me to join the group.

First Impressions: At the first meeting I became one of nine sheepish women, united only by Yvonne and a common AT&T history. We were each intrigued, but our expectations unformed. None of us was sure why she was there. Certainly my attendance was a tentative step. I knew I was burned-out, and wasn't yet anxious to work, but I could imagine, maybe, a life beyond leisure. Dana said, "I came because Yvonne told me." We all smiled at her candor, her willingness to admit something that was probably true for all of us. Yvonne had originally described the proposed group as "talented and high-powered women" saying, "it was a waste not to use these talents in a positive way." I agreed with this assessment.

Fran and Judy inspired me. I'd been lolling around in frivolous pursuits, while, after long careers, they had both discovered their passions. Fran had become a botanical artist even though she had never drawn seriously until after her retirement. I confess I had feelings of envy, since I had not one artistic bone in my body. The day Fran said, "I think I have a deal" – she had licensed her drawings for a china pattern – we all cheered. And then there was Judy, an aspiring writer. Judy told us that she devoted the first two hours of every day to her writing. Her commitment made me yearn to not just get a life, but to get a meaningful life.

Sometimes I felt guilty that my life had so little focus, but I reminded myself that I didn't have to be competitive about my leisure or retirement. I told myself that finding a new path takes time and I deserved the luxury of living a life without other's expectations clouding my decisions. I thought about Judy and Fran and convinced myself that it had taken them time to find their new avocations.

On the lighter side, my life did provide some humor to the group. I was asked, "Are you still cleaning out your attic?" It was suggested that I might have found a new career since it had taken me twenty-five years to fill that attic. (More about the attic cleaning later.) I became the self-appointed pop culture guru, the result of my hours of endless television viewing. The day I quoted Dr. Phil, Fran screamed, "Kathy, how could you?"

Identity crisis: While visiting my dermatologist's office, I was asked to complete a new patient form. Confronted with the question, "Career?" I paused for a second, gulped and wrote Retired. When recounting this incident at our next meeting, I was surprised when Yvonne promptly chirped "self-employed" and Margaret Ann suggested "on sabbatical."

All of us had defined our existence in terms of our career. For us the R-word did not flow easily from our lips. Suddenly, I realized that I could be "retired" for as many years as I'd worked – more than 30 years. What a revelation! No wonder I was searching for something meaningful to fill the rest of my days. The other eight women were on a similar search.

From Fire Island to "Drawing on the Right Side of the Brain": We were returning from our first adventure, our excursion to Fire Island, in Yvonne's BMW. Driving 85 mph on the Long Island Expressway with the radar detector often beeping, I listened to Fran rave about a wonderful new approach to art. She suggested that everyone could find her artistic talent by drawing a figure upside-down. Simultaneous hoots and guffaws erupted from Margaret Ann and Yvonne. Yvonne said, "I can't draw and I don't think anyone can teach me how." Margaret Ann said, "I'm worse!" I thought to myself, "But I am the worst!"

Two months later we were all on Carol's deck on a beautiful autumn day, telling our recruited teacher that she wouldn't be able to teach us to draw. Three days later, we had each completed five drawings. Amazed at my new ability, I'd drawn one of my hands, a cup and saucer, the face of a woman in an ad, a perspective of a planter on Carol's deck, and a self-portrait. They were all recognizable. Although Fran's drawing of the cup and saucer was delicate, fine porcelain china, in contrast, mine was diner-fare, heavy pottery, slightly uneven, probably a second. Nevertheless, my dinerware could be identified as a cup and saucer. Fran, Dana and Duffy were the stars of this workshop. They were talented and had experience. Their works were quite remarkable. Carol surprised herself by drawing a terrific self-portrait. Yvonne, Margaret Ann and I, still jokingly vying for the title of the "worst," were secretly pleased with our own successes.

This group drawing course was a turning point for me, and maybe for all nine of us. In my family, my younger brother was artistic and encouraged to develop his talent, and I, who had no talent, was encouraged to do other things, like study. I had to force myself to participate in the art course; I would never have chosen it by myself; and I don't think I was alone in my reaction. Each of us took a risk in participating. For those of us who'd started out with no experience, our risk was of looking foolish, while for those who were artistic, their risk was apprehension over producing great drawings. For an "overachieving" group of women, the fear of failure is a strong emotion, not easily overcome. At the end of the three days, all of us had a wonderful sense of accomplishment. This adventure was filled with apprehension, anxiety, laughter, learning, and friendship –our group of nine women "bonded" while creating a context for expanding our lives by doing unexpected things.

Nine Women and Their Stories (The Career Chronicles): I was always enamored of our pet project "the history of the foot soldiers in the feminist revolution". After all I was (and am) a feminist and I had been a history major in college. But what started as a fact-driven, questionnaire-focused exercise magically transformed into a way for nine women to share the stories of their lives and careers. Sometimes it reminded me of my consciousness-raising group in the early 1970's. The "all-female" environment, the openness and the honesty were similar, but it was also different. Instead of struggling with the big issues of feminism, we in fact were simply talking about the things that made us who we are today, probing how we got to be the way we are, but with no apologies. Sometimes, it was a bit like a soap opera. As "The Days of Our Lives" rolled across an imaginary screen, a topic would get queued up, someone would tell their story and then a second person would chime in, and then a third person and then a fourth person – and so on – a virtual free-for-all of stories and emotions. The energy was contagious and the end result amazing. I found the sessions thoroughly therapeutic, allowing myself a way to look back over my life and my career, and to recall the memories – the good and the bad. I discovered that I was not alone; I learned that eight other women shared my feelings, experiences, and emotions. Somehow, there was healing in the storytelling, I was ready to put my past to bed and to move on with my life.

Life beyond leisure: The last eighteen months have been a time of renewal for me. I no longer feel like a clandestine bum. I've regained the energy my career had sapped and I have adhered to many of the essentials from my first month of leisure: living a healthy life, reading voraciously, cooking, and exercising. I am still "cleaning out my attic," but now I am doing it as a forerunner to the renovation of my old 1830 era home. I find that cleaning out my attic is not only a physical activity but also a metaphor for sorting through my life. I am deciding what I treasure and want to keep and what is no longer needed. I am learning to let go and move on.

Following Fran's advice, I've become a follower of the tenets of *The Artist's Way* by Julia Cameron, a structured approach to achieving creativity. I keep a journal and use the recommended "Artist Dates" as a source of energy and pleasure. On one such Artist Date, walking along the Delaware Canal near my home in Pennsylvania, I was enjoying the early spring day and snapping pictures with my digital camera. Suddenly I spotted two beavers (I'd never seen these furry creatures before.) They swam and frolicked in the canal, then slapped the water with their fat tails and dove. It was a delightful moment.

My walks allow me time to reflect. Like many of the women in our group, I had wanted to be financially independent and a success. I am proud of the life I created; achieving not only my dreams but also surpassing my parents' aspirations. Thinking about the Thomas Szasz quote, I had "created" a self that was a strong successful executive. Now, I accept that this chapter of my life is closed. It is time for a new creation.

I know that my future will be very different from my past. When I left corporate America I promised myself that I would stop doing things that I was good at, but that I did not enjoy. I also promised that I would no longer work or socialize with people that I did not like or respect. As Jeanne Ray writes in *Eat Cake*:

> "Sometimes you have time to sort it all through. Is it enough to just find a job that will take the place of my other job? I'll tell you, Ruth, I think about it now and I'm not so sure I was happy in the other job. I think I was just on autopilot the whole time. I don't want to go

back to that life. I want to try and figure out what I'm supposed to do, what I might be good at. I really want to be good at something, to feel passionate about it."

Maybe it is the celestine prophecy at work, but I see signs urging me to pursue something I love everywhere I look. I saw an interview with Julia Child, at 90 years of age, she said, "I will never retire, because I love what I do." I read an article about Al Hirschfeld who worked as an artist till the day he died at 99. He said, "I can't imagine not working." Pam sent us an email about Po Bronson's book *What Should I Do With My Life?*, a book about people who chose to pursue their dreams. Oprah, showcasing some of these people, told her audience, "Follow your heart." And Dr. Phil – yes, laugh if you must, but I still watch him on occasion – urges his audience to "Follow your passion" and "Find your authentic self." He reminds us that who we are is not what we do. Julia Cameron talks about synchronicity and advises us to "take a small step in the direction of a dream and watch the synchronous doors flying open." She believes that if we are committed to a dream we will find the means to achieve it.

For thirty years my unrelenting focus on financial and professional success suppressed any other desires. As a professional woman, I felt alone, an outsider whose only support came from my husband. Reliving my life and the lives of the other eight women in the group during "our career chronicles," I realized that I have many more dreams to fulfill. So what is to be my life beyond leisure?

I love to cook, but I don't want to be a chef.

I like strength training, but I don't want to be a fitness trainer.

I love volunteering at my local library, but I don't want to be a librarian.

I love books; do I want to be a writer?

I love digital photography; do I want to be a photographer?

I do know that whatever I do will be a creative enterprise. Maybe I will become a photo essayist. Maybe I'll help others who want to find their creative selves as they retire or move on to second careers.

In this journey I do know that I will have the support and friendship of eight women with whom I have laughed and cried and who are on their own journeys. With this group, I am an "insider" and I look forward to our adventures together.

An Adventuress On The Hunt

Duffy Kopriva

Two weeks after my birth I was christened Margaret Mary; at the age of twelve, in a moment of religious fervor, I added Theresa as my confirmation name. *Margaret Mary Theresa.* With a name like that I was destined to be either a fiery redheaded rebellious, hell-on-wheels adolescent or a demure, mousy-brown-haired, goody-two-shoes type of kid – no in-between. Darned if I didn't turn out to be that shy, quiet, good kid; one

144

of the brainy kids in my small town school. I missed a lot of good times because of that. To make matters worse, I had matchstick thin legs that were a perfect fit for my skinny, pencil-thin figure and perched on my nose were unfashionable pink glasses – a geek before the term was born.

By the time I left my little burg for college, I was fed up with Margaret Mary, ready for a complete makeover, wanting desperately to be a different me. Over time contact lenses replaced the glasses, an eating campaign of five meals a day added pounds, enabling me to break the 100-pound barrier and add a curve or two, my cute little dresses were stored away in favor of slacks, and I began practicing a variety of flirting techniques in the mirror and occasionally on a real guy. Ah yes, I also changed my name – out with Margaret Mary and in with Duffy. Okay, so it wasn't the best choice of names and I hadn't considered that I would be called Duffy for the remainder of my adult life. To the ears of an eighteen-year-old, Duffy, sounded fun-loving, cute, and a bit sexy.

Sometimes, even after all this time, the confidence fades and that shy, awkward Margaret Mary Theresa shows up. And darned if a bit of her wasn't there at the first meeting of the group. I wondered how an entrepreneur might fit into this assembly of corporate women. After all, hadn't they all worked together at AT&T for most or all of their careers, lunched with each other and shared the thrill of promotions or exotic business trips, and, on the bad days, the painful frustration of working for an inept boss or getting assigned to a loser of a project. While I, needing to spread my business wings and be master of my own sink-or-swim venture, had left the corporate world of AT&T eighteen years earlier to seek my fortune as an entrepreneur.

Being an entrepreneur was in my genes. My father and his father and my maternal grandfather were all independent business owners. Periodically, someone will comment to me that I was brave to leave the safe haven of a big company and venture into the turbulent and, though they are too polite to say it - much less prestigious arena of small business. It wasn't bravery; it was tunnel vision. I just knew that I wanted to run my own company. For several years before I made the move to leave AT&T to start my own business, the glorious Holy Grail of being a business owner blazed before me. But those years passed with no action, causing a number of lectures to myself about procrastination. Then, *eureka*! The kick in the proverbial butt – AT&T initiated the first of their downsizing efforts, the first of many that would come over the next fifteen years.

Downsizing and right-sizing became common place in the late-1980's and 1990's, but at this point-in-time, it was foreign and strange – many people stayed with one company for years and often for their entire work life. Despite a healthy financial incentive to leave, managers all around me were shrinking from the thought of giving up their hard won positions, while I, wild with enthusiasm, rushed to sign the documents, thinking that fourteen good years in the corporate world was enough. Heady with anticipation, I went home to tell my husband of the new direction in our lives. Both of us had visions of different careers, and fortunately I'm married to an understanding man who laughed that I beat him out the door.

AT&T, which trained its people well, was a wonderful place for a young person in the early 1970's to learn about business. Data processing was in its infancy then and being hired as a systems programmer I was given an opportunity to hold responsible positions early in my career. Enjoying change, I moved around the company and over the years managed a variety of projects and led groups in information systems, engineering and marketing. With each job change came new skills, business acumen and knowledge. My last position at AT&T was in the marketing department as the Division Manager of General Business Systems, translate small business. It was especially appropriate for the direction my career was taking and provided me an extra dose of self-assurance.

So, as I launched my entrepreneurial quest, I was exuberant, loaded with confidence and energy. After evaluating several business ideas, I settled on putting together a private women's club. This would be a place where professional women could gather for exercise, grooming, dining, a cocktail and good conversation with like-minded women. I labored on this project for months raising the necessary capital (convincing bankers, finding investors, etc), forming a membership and creating financial statements by the truckload. Over the months my enthusiasm waned as I slowly faced up to the realization that it just wasn't going to work. Location was critical and the right one couldn't be found. I also became convinced that women, although they loved the idea of their own sanctuary, were too busy with careers and raising families to have the time and the money for the luxury of a private club. And most importantly, it was wrong for me; a club focuses on meeting personal needs for individuals, whereas I was learning that my strengths and preferences lie in the business-to-business world.

The lessons learned from my efforts would be invaluable in the future and I now consider them my MBA in entrepreneurship. But, that was a delayed revelation and first I had to deal with the disappointment and grief of my failure, which is exactly what it seemed to be to me. It took me much too long to let go of my vision, even when I knew I must. Devastated and depressed, I moped about trying to get my feet back on solid ground. With the help of husband, family and friends I survived, patched up my ego, and began looking for another opportunity.

After what seemed a very long wait at the time, I learned of HQ Business Centers and it seemed a good fit for my talents. In this industry, offices, telephone service, conference rooms, staff, the whole array of office needs are offered as a turn-key solution to businesses needing relatively small amounts of sophisticated office space. What drew me to HQ was that each owner was responsible for managing their total business, from securing office space, overseeing the build-out of the space, raising capital, putting together ad campaigns, setting prices, sending out billing, and hiring staff, to creating pensions plans and expanding their businesses.

Looking forward to running my own business, I partnered with a local businessman and we opened an executive suite in New Jersey. The business was good, but the partnership wasn't. After a year we ended the business arrangement. I now had 100% ownership and 100% responsibility for the company. It was my baby. Soon I added another center in New Jersey and then one in Jacksonville, Florida. The Jacksonville expansion not only opened a growing market but enabled my husband and me to live there half the year escaping the cold northern winters.

The business was a joy for me (most days), and over ten years, like many business owners, I gave it extraordinary amounts of time and energy. In return it provided a multitude of new learning experiences. Sometimes it forced me to action when I would have preferred to hide in bed. By doing what I feared, I soon learned that I could muster the courage to do most anything that was required to keep my company healthy. I negotiated long-term real estate leases with hard-boiled building owners, evaluated and purchased large-scale communications equipment, moved forty client offices and my operation to a new office building over a weekend to avoid lost business time, and called company presidents to demand action when failing equipment their companies had sold me caused serious business problems. I had plenty of opportunities to make decisions and test business theory in the real world to my heart's content.

Running your own business is a bit like having a restless, mischievous elf residing on your shoulder. Ever so often, the little fellow nods off and you get some peace, but much of the time he raises a dickens getting into all manner of devilment, wrecking havoc on many a good day and quite a few nights. Once, having invited three of my friends to be my guests for a day of golf, the elf acted up, serious equipment problems arose, and much to my dismay, the golf game had to go on without me. To make matters worse, while I owned the business I don't think I went on a single vacation where I really relaxed. I must have been a bit crazy to enjoy this environment, but I did.

In the late 1990's, a large company came wooing the HQ owners offering to buy their businesses. After the women's club experience, I had learned my lesson about letting go. This was a golden apple of an opportunity and if not plucked in a timely manner it would disappear.

After six months of grueling intensity during which negotiations were conducted, a purchase price established, and mountains of due diligence paperwork accumulated, I sold my centers and was set free.

I was fifty years old. Now what would I do? My friends, believing the lure and excitement of business life would capture and pull me back, predicted that I'd be involved in another entrepreneurial venture in no time. I knew that I wanted a year to relax, but I thought they were right, that I would find a new business and in short order be leading the hectic, exciting life I had just left. We were wrong! It's been five years now and I see that moving on to new experiences is where the excitement lies.

For me, the enjoyment of retirement has been a chance to explore interests long ignored. I love the outdoors. Is it possible that most of my adult life was misspent trapped inside an office? Making up for lost time, I kayak for hours paddling on rivers, lakes and coastal waterways with my binoculars draped about my neck, ever ready for the chance to see a bird that is new to me or one that I especially enjoy watching. I'm slowly learning as many bird songs and calls as I my non-musical ears and brain will retain. I stare up at trees, crouch down to examine flowers, butterflies and beetles, and peer into streams to absorb what nature has to teach me. Playing golf is my husband's passion and I love the time we spend on the course together. He is good-natured about the binoculars I smuggle into the golf cart in order to better observe the baby red tail hawks that are squealing for lunch high in the ancient pine tree on the third hole. Because I really do enjoy business and am afraid my brain will atrophy in its absence, I dabble in various endeavors, from investing in real estate to helping others start businesses. I even acted as a COO of a small firm for a short period of time. Fun with family and friends, travel, good books, new experiences, observing and commenting on our world and the historical changes we are experiencing, just having time for the many things that were pushed aside in my previous life, all of these make this time of my life rich and wonderful. I think of myself as an adventuress on the hunt. I'm doing my best not to miss a thing.

NineWomen appeals to me. It is yet another opportunity for exploration and growth. These energetic, fun-loving women are like magnets. What could be better than exchanging ideas with bright, accomplished women for the purpose of achieving a worthwhile goal? I subscribe to the theory of "use it or lose it"; it's important to stay mentally alert by pushing one's self to think in a disciplined and creative way, to identify goals and put a plan in place to achieve it. The problem is this – from experience I know that any successful effort (business or otherwise) takes extraordinary amounts of time, energy and devotion. As a self-proclaimed adventuress I want time for my other pursuits and am no longer willing to take on the full-time commitment that a business requires. With the group, however, there's the opportunity to share the workload, yet still pursue creative, worthwhile projects, enjoy the mental gymnastics of problem-solving, and partner with women whom I admire and enjoy. Now that's a great concept.

I needn't have worried about fitting into the group. Even at our first meeting the room was charged with energy, talk, excitement, questions, answers, catching up, introductions and, best of all, good will. I loved the diversity of the group right from the beginning, both personalities and interests. Energetic Fran with her beautiful botanical art, intellectual Judy with her accomplished writing and, insightful Margaret Ann with her vivid photography were so accomplished in their new avocations; I was wowed. Erudite Kathy, recently retired, made us laugh with her descriptions of cleaning her attic, a project that was likely to occupy her time for the better part of a year or perhaps the rest of her life if she didn't speed the process up. Carol's daughter plays in the high school band and Carol, caring and generous, had bravely volunteered to prepare a meal for the parents of the band members, all 200 of them. Daring Dana was happily dancing from one pastime to another, experimenting. Career-minded Pam (a thinker and doer) and Yvonne (creativity in action) were thinking about what would be next in their pursuit of new challenges. Here were eight strong women reinventing themselves for Act II of their lives. It was easy to like them all immediately. I was hooked. I wanted to know these women and be a part of what they created.

The reach of the group goes far beyond our stated purpose. For like Dana, at this point in my life, I have a strong desire to strengthen friendships and make new ones. *NineWomen* offers a unique opportunity to act on this. My life as an entrepreneur in the executive suite business had been lonely in a number of ways. First, no matter how close you are to your employees, suppliers, bankers, and advisors, the management of the company is solely your responsibility. You struggle with complex decisions knowing that making a really bad one can bring the company down, cost people their jobs and put you in debt deeper than twenty leagues under the cold, dark sea. Alone with your fears, you take the risk, make the decision and implement as carefully as you can. In the group we are nine women each with our own views and opinions, but united for a common purpose and goal. We discuss, we air-our-views, we take positions, but the underlying camaraderie and support that I longed for as an entrepreneur is alive and well.

By being with these women as each uniquely redefines herself, I'm seeing options available to me that I would not have considered without them. With Judy's encouragement, I attended a writing workshop at Sarah Lawrence College and now my 87 year-old mother and I are joyfully recording her early years so this precious piece of family history is not lost. This summer, because of Fran and our famous drawing class, I am continuing my art education – botanical drawing of course. It's fun, no pressure to be Rembrandt, just the pleasure of exploring. When I need a jump-start of the mind I call Yvonne. She is forever coming up with out-of-the-box thinking that grabs my brain cells by their roots and shakes them into action. If I have a medical question or need to do some research, I ask Kathy, who is a wealth of knowledge and know-how. Margaret Ann, our resident photography and computer guru, gives me tips on the best color printer and how to make the computer enhance digital photography. The individual and the collective wisdom of the group is awesome and lucky for me; it's there for the asking.

Over the twenty months since our first meeting, we have evolved as a group and as a team. Initially, having endured thirty years of deadlines, schedules and due dates, we luxuriated in the leisurely exploration of any topic that was of interest and became happily immersed in meandering conversations, not to be held accountable for any specific result. A little more than a year after we started meeting, the time was right for a specific project, complete with assignments and due dates. The booklet was born.

The "booklet" was the name we gave the project which resulted in this book. We called it a booklet because it was too intimidating to think about doing something bigger. "Let's just do a booklet," Judy encouragingly said, luring us to action. Business writing was our forte; composing a book of essays would be an entirely different and a much more challenging endeavor. Having tested our aptitude for taking on unfamiliar territory with the "Drawing on the Right Side of the Brain" art class, we were about to push the envelope of our comfort zones again and begin writing. None of us, save Judy, has any formal training in writing. Thus Judy, with no way out, became our leader on this project. She is a gentle coach and along the way she brought in two pros, Cheryl Harris Sharman and Penny Wolfson to guide, critique and encourage us, without whose help this book would have been a different animal if it existed at all. A major piece of their advice was *add emotion*. Business writing is noted for its lack of sentiment and we all had years of experience meeting that criteria. Now we were being told to do the opposite. Interesting essays demanded emotional content, we were told. Back to our PCs, we twisted and fidgeted until the feelings turned into words, hopefully allowing you the reader to know us as real people.

From the very beginning many of our discussions revolved around supporting women – women in business, women in retirement, women of all ages and generations experiencing many different types of transitions. We discussed the possibility of setting up a forum for women of different generations to communicate. The well being, success, advancement, and self-realization of women is an abiding interest of ours. When it became obvious how much our group meant to us and how it was enhancing this stage of our lives, it occurred to us that it was worth sharing. Could our approach to teamwork and cooperative projects be of interest and assistance to other women who were entering retirement and wanted to remain vital and continue making contributions? And if other women formed groups similar to ours, couldn't we set up a dialogue among ourselves? And might not younger women like to give their views on their successes and their struggles? Perhaps the reason for our coming together was in our very own backyard. By writing a book about our group experience perhaps we could inspire other women who are redefining their lives or considering how to do so to join us. By working together and sharing ideas even greater horizons could be reached.

We had been in the initial wave of women pursuing full-time careers. Now we are on the forefront of career women entering retirement. As we explore this new phase of our lives, we want it to be just as defining and successful as our careers, but with a more creative and balanced definition of success. Unfortunately retirement is a word that sends the wrong message, for we are not slacking off in the least. All of us are exploring fulfilling new ways to use our talents and myriad of skills. Pam, already at her new job, gave us an update on the corporate world at our meeting to name this book. Dana and her family have arrived in Ireland to live there for a year; Yvonne has spent the day at a challenging part-time work assignment that still allows time for her golf game; and Carol has put her writing projects aside in order to spend some very important time with good friends. Priorities have shifted, giving our real personalities and interests time to blossom.

Thirty years ago, a person over fifty was considered old by many – thank goodness times have changed. A new model for maturing is given by Claire Braz-Valentine, a poet and writer. She writes, *"My fantasy of aging is to age well enough so that younger women would think*, Gee, I wish I were her age. *I want the stigma of aging to be removed from women. So, for all those younger women and for myself, I intend to do it with as much panache as I can. I'm going to put everything I've got into it."*

Let's put everything we got into it. With living to be one-hundred-years-old not out of question, at fifty-something, we are just beginning. In contrast to our business lives, what we have to contribute this time can be accomplished in our own image, without the constraints of business protocol, and not as isolated figures, but as women in our prime, working our magic with the support of wise and good friends. As I peer into the future, the grand design may be hazy, but what is clear is that *NineWomen* is an important ingredient to the richness of the journey.

An Unfinished Story

Excited about the positive impact the group had already made in our lives, we wanted to inspire other women to form groups like ours. Our purpose: to enrich women's lives by creating a powerful network of groups that stimulate dialogue among women, working and retired, to identify common areas of interest and perhaps join forces in joint projects. In early April, 2003 we decided to write and distribute a pamphlet.

Judy suggested that the members of the group each write a personal essay discussing how the group impacted our lives. Shudders ran around the room -- no one else had ever written a personal essay. Our group rarely backs away from a challenge. "Just a short one," Dana said.

We were surprised at the resulting thoughtful commentaries that emerged. Carol realized how much she, and the rest of us, had consistently underestimated our individual capabilities. She wanted to challenge herself, and all women, to develop the kind of self-confidence justified by our accomplishments and talents. Kathy's story encouraged risk-taking and pushed women to realize their dreams. Pam chose to reach women who were still actively involved in their careers, but going through a tough transition in these economic times; she wanted to let them know there are other women who felt the same way they did. Fran wanted other women to know that our group sometimes ran into serious communication problems, but, at least so far, we'd been able to resolve them. Yvonne wanted our readers to realize they are incredibly talented, and that they can make a real difference in people's lives.

Seeing something good, our group often reacts by wanting it to be better. We asked Cheryl Harris Sharman to edit our work. A contributing editor for Prism Magazine, a regular reviewer for the Miami Herald, and a former columnist for

Central America's *Tico* Times, Cheryl is now working with an agent on her own book. At the beginning of the next set of meetings, someone would be walking around the room, excitedly sharing the comments she'd received from Cheryl with the others. We each went back to our computers, struggling to cleanup our sentence structure and develop our thoughts.

We decided to include a few of the sketches we did in the drawing class we took with Mindy Lighthipe, an artist who is also the coordinator for the Botanical Art and Illustration program at the New York Botanical Garden and the co-founder of the Academy for Natural Arts. Fran added a botanical sketch. Because a few of us are blossoming photographers, we also printed some of our better camera shots. We started calling our efforts a "booklet."

As we lounged on a deck at Long Beach Island in June, Kathy said, "I feel that the booklet is almost great." Later, as we were investigating publication, Fran worried that we still didn't have a story that would be interesting to others. So we asked Penny Wolfson to lead a one-day writing workshop. We held this day long session – yes, at a Corporate Headquarters building. Penny teaches writing to graduate students at Sarah Lawrence, has won a National Magazine Award in Feature Writing, had her writing included in Best Essays 2002, and is the author of a book called *MOONRISE: One Family, Genetic Identity, and Muscular Dystrophy*. She started the day with a discussion of what we were trying to achieve. Then, while each of us held one-on-one meetings with Penny to get her comments on our essays, the rest of the group wrote down our goals for the booklet.

We returned to our computers with renewed energy. Penny had told us to tell more about our early days at work and to share more of our feelings. "You all back away from emotion," she said. We laughed. We'd spent multi-decade careers learning to hide our real feelings. We let our emotions rip (or at least that's how we felt). Those of us who hadn't told much about their early lives and careers significantly expanded their essays.

Judy wanted other women to understand her misgivings as she re-evaluated her career and to get the kind of support she'd received from the group. Dana, who had moved with her family to Ireland for a year, wanted to inspire women as they faced the uncertain future of transition and proceeded to Act II of their lives. Margaret Ann hoped that other women would benefit from hearing her new-found definition of success.

Duffy, who enjoys kayaking with her binoculars poised and supports environmental efforts, wanted to ignite women to join in small groups like ours to have fun, but also to pursue causes that will make the world a better place to live.

With Penny's encouragement, Fran agreed to write an introduction, Yvonne started working on her discussion of our group processes, and Duffy and Judy agreed to collaborate on a summary. The next time we surveyed the results, we had more than180 pages. We'd written a book!

Kathy became enthused about a marketing approach. Margaret Ann and Fran started working on graphics. Duffy and Carol put together a business plan. Pam held an evening meeting at her house to "greenlight" ideas for a new name for our group and the book's name. We registered our group's new name. At the end of September we sent *Beyond the Corner Office -- Essays by NineWomen* to "press," as they say in the trade.

Then in October, 2003 FORTUNE magazine ran an article about women and power. We took particular interest in the article because many of us had worked for or with the woman named the most powerful in business (Carly

Fiorina), the woman with the highest salary (Pat Russo), and one of the women quoted for her ideas about the future (Gail McGovern). In her article Patricia Sellers said that many of the powerful women she interviewed said they "don't want to be Carly Fiorina and . . . run a huge company." She asked: "Do women lack power in business because they don't want it enough?"

Our group realized we had something to consider about an important issue. We need to delve deeper into why all of us left the corporate world at an early age, and to discuss whether we agree with Harvard Business School Professor Gail McGovern who was quoted in the Fortune article as saying that "young men and women will start to change the face of business – eventually creating a level playing field that's more attractive to women." By tackling things we would normally have shied away from, we have increased our confidence and provided a safe environment for even more profound discussion. Fran said, "Maybe we should start a dialogue about today's corporate climate and how it is satisfying, or not satisfying, the needs of women."

We knew the FORTUNE article was just one example of events that will continue to impact our thoughts and actions. Then another bombshell arrived in our mailboxes. Both AT&T and Lucent, the companies that provide benefits for many of us, are reducing their medical benefits. This process is widespread. In 1993 40% of employers provided medical benefits; in 2001, 20%. And other companies, like the ones we depend on, are not eliminating them, but drastically reducing them. We worry about the implications of these actions for us, our families, and the larger population retired people. We are interested in becoming a catalyst for change. These problems-needing-solutions can unite us so that we can collectively take action when that seems to be the right approach.

All fired up, we agreed to update this summary when we received our book galley. Duffy said, "The power of an individual group like ours will be increased if we start now to facilitate information exchange, leading to opportunities for greater change." Our work-in-progress will be continued, because the issues that we are talking about are critical to women and to society, and because each of us continues to grow.

We would love to hear from you - whether you are interested in forming a group, already have one, have a story to tell, a thought that must be shared, or just have a question to ask. Tell us what women's issues you think are significant today, and what you or your group are doing.

Because we have found such joy and reward in our group we are eager to assist you in setting up yours. Your group does not have to be a carbon copy of ours, your group should follow your passions and explore your desired futures. The resource material located in Part II of the book will help you form your own group if you so desire. We've provided our questionnaire as a starting point. We would really like to encourage you to use the questionnaire as a guide to exploring your past and as a way to share your experiences the people in your own group and with us.

While we've have also described our principles of operation, the sequence of events that we felt were fundamental to the success of our group, and the valuable lessons we learned along the way, we only mean to provide guideposts that you can move or take down.

We would love to have your responses Based on responses from a wide range of women of all ages and career paths, we hope to see some very interesting trends and perhaps create a dialogue across the generations. We want to keep in touch with you via email, and perhaps through a website and another book.

You can reach us at *NineWomen@att.net*.

Resources:
Looking Through The Rear View Mirror

As we look back at how NineWomen evolved, we realize that there were a lot of things we did right – and some things we would change if we started again tomorrow. This section offers some thoughts and recommendations for other women who are thinking about forming their own groups.

We want to help you organize and run your group so that you can benefit from what we have learned. The process we used is not an academic ritual nor is it a "how to" that can be followed blindly. Our recommendations provide guidelines, suggestions, things to consider, questions to ask, and are offered in goodwill, so others can benefit from our experiences.

Before you start, we suggest you think about your motivation for starting the group. The group may eventually change its direction, but you should have an articulated objective for bringing the group together. For example, do you want to be part of a nationwide group that engages in an Across-the-Generations conversation? Or do you want to pursue a specific project area, like healthcare insurance for the baby boomers? Do you want to pursue "for profit" projects or do your interests lie in the not for profit area?

In our group, we wanted to pursue a project to improve the quality of life for women like us, have the opportunity to make it a profitable venture, and have fun doing it! . We were not very specific and this has given us the freedom to explore many different areas. Over the eighteen months since we started our initial motivation has been revised somewhat but continues to provide guidance for our efforts.

Deciding on size of group and how to choose members:

1.   The group size should be no greater than ten and no smaller than six. You want to have enough people so that you can get meaningful discussion and

exchange of ideas, yet you need to keep it intimate and manageable. Our group has nine women and at an average meeting we have six women participate.

2.   The women should be strong and capable women. This is not intended to be group therapy! Every member of the group should materially contribute to what the group does.

3.   If possible, it helps to have common backgrounds, interests, and/or values. In our group, we all had worked at AT&T or one of its spin-offs, retired at a young age, and were actively involved in the Feminist Revolution of the 70's.

4.   It is important to have individuals who value the pursuit of truth above "being right."

Making decisions about meetings- where, how often, and how they are run:

1.   We recommend meeting in a rented facility. This supports the objective that this is not a social-only gathering, but rather you are meeting to accomplish group-defined goals. It also relieves group members of the need to "hostess" meetings. You will need to raise money to

pay for the facilities, unless you can get a church or someplace that would be willing to provide the space without pay. We meet at a rented facility and pay an average of $100.00 per meeting.

2. All group members are equal. We have been women in the workforce used to being "the boss"; therefore it works best for us to use a process where everyone has accountability for what happens in the group.

3. Name a facilitator to be the central point of contact, guide the group through discussions, keep continuity of direction, and document meeting decisions and agreements. We started with Yvonne being the facilitator and she did this for over a year. Then we have been alternating the role of facilitator – Carol, Kathy, and Duffy. We think it is best to keep the same facilitator for at least the first year. This provides continuity at a time when the group is starting to "gel". After the first year, the role should be rotated, but it should be voluntary. And it should be for a period of at least 3 months.

We have tried rotating in a more "ad hoc" way and it has caused some confusion.

4.   Meet every two to three weeks. This keeps the interest growing without making it a "chore." There have been times when we have met more frequently than that, on as needed basis, but overall the 2-3 weeks works well.

5.   The meeting should not last over 3 hours. We have experimented with longer meetings (all day) and they bring with them all of the evils of all-day meetings we had experienced in the corporate world. Keeping meetings short was a key lesson for us.

6.   While you should have an agenda for the meeting, allow it to be flexible to include topics for discussion rather than too many specific action items. You want to keep the meetings exciting and inspiring and when they deteriorate to reviewing to-do lists, they become boring and feel like "work." The facilitator walks a fine line between getting items discussed and allowing spontaneous discussions.

7.   Lastly, you should definitely record the agreements reached at the meeting and any other information that would be helpful in keeping track of the group progress. This should be sent out to all members and need not be detailed but should contain the important information.

Getting started:

1.   It works well to first discuss why people are interested in joining the group.   What are their expectations? What are their concerns, if any?

2.   It is important to develop a set of principles for the group. We did this during our first meeting, addressing issues such as having fun, encouraging ideas, becoming a women-only group, and defining intellectual property around business ideas.

3.   Let the group determine areas of interest. It will be very important that it does not become a task-oriented only group. The topics should encourage exploration and incorporate intellectual, emotional, social, and developmental dimensions. We started with a discussion

of business ideas, which evolved into a discussion of topics of interest to us. From these discussions, the idea of helping others create groups like ours emerged. This process will take some time. We explored different areas for about nine months before we coalesced on a project. Be patient with the each other and enjoy the process!

Coming together: The process we follow is best described as an ad-hoc, organic process, where conversations and areas of interest move us to common areas of interest. The meetings provide minimal structure to allow the group members to get to know each other and to deepen the trust among us.

1.   We start every meeting with a check-in of what is in people's minds. Everyone participates and we go around the room. Keep it short -- no more than 10 minutes per person. This allows everyone to get to know each other. We share our worries and our delights, and have the opportunity to speak what is on our minds.   At times, we exceed the time allotted, and that is fine, occasionally.

2.   It is important to develop trust among the group members. This is needed in order for individuals to feel comfortable taking risks, which, in turn, is necessary in the creative process. In our group, since not everyone knew each other, we planned an outing where its explicit purpose was to get to know each other better. We went on an overnight stay to a beautiful place – Fire Island – and we traveled, cooked, ate, drank, and played together. All that was required was to talk with each other as we saw fit and to enjoy the beautiful scenery. This worked very well for us. One could feel the energy emerging from this outing! We then decided to incorporate periodic activities that would allow us to have fun and share learning, good food and good times.

3.   Plan a shared learning experience. When people feel vulnerable and the group offers support, it helps develop trust in each other. Learning experiences provide personal as well as group growth opportunities, and both have been important for our group. We took the *Drawing on the Right Side of the*

Brain class together. While not everyone was taking the same risk, everyone felt "exposed," and the support from the group was instrumental in getting the group to move forward.

4. Design an instrument that allows the group to develop a deeper level of relationship and stimulates meaningful discussion. We developed a questionnaire (included in the next section) to do this. The impact of the questionnaire was twofold. While we designed the questions, we discussed what was important to us. As we discussed our personal answers to the questions, each of us spoke about things that we had not articulated before. Not only did this prove to be worthwhile time spent because it brought clarity to us as individuals but it also cemented the group relationship. If you decide to use a questionnaire (which we recommend) you can use our version as it stands or you can develop your own and use ours to see if there is anything you forgot that is important to you.

5. Periodically, spend time together in a beautiful place (we also went

to Long Beach Island) to just be together, having fun. We find that this keeps the energy flowing and reminds the group of how much we enjoy each other's company.

Dealing with conflict: There will be times when the group disagrees or when someone in the group feels they are not being heard or when an individual feels frustrated with the time it takes to make a decision…or many other reasons. We have experienced several of these situations.

1. When this happens, the facilitator should take the lead and raise the issue for everyone to know it is happening. Many times, misunderstandings happen because people are not aware of what they are doing and the effect it may be having on others.

2. If the facilitator is unaware of what is happening, or unable to deal with it, then someone else in the group should step up to the challenge. A key attribute of a self-managed group is that everyone in the group is accountable for its ongoing health.

3.   One technique we frequently used was discussing our preferred styles of interaction, whether we are introverts or extroverts, whether we are intuitive or data driven, etc. The important thing is to de-personalize the problem and put it in the context of the different ways people interact.

4.   Be explicit about what could be done to avoid the same problem in the future. Sometimes, there is nothing that can be done, but more times than not, there are things that can be done. An example from our experience was that some people felt we were constantly revisiting our decisions and thus wasting a lot of our time together. When we looked at this we realized that this was partly due because we lacked clarity in articulating when a decision was made. So we decided to make decisions explicit. And that has worked well for us.

5.   Above all, remember what brought you together and take the high road whenever you have the opportunity!

And last but not least: Make sure that some part of every meeting includes fun. For our group, often planning a fun outing was fun. Sometimes we took time out for a celebration of a member's success.

Now you are ready to start your group. In the business world, one would have objectives and a plan to accomplish those objectives before getting started. We found out that there is more than one way to get things done. The beauty of our approach is that we can define next steps as we go. The most important learning we can share is to take it a step at a time ... and the most important advice is to take the time to enjoy this wonderful process!

Resources:
The Questionnaire

We completed this questionnaire individually first and shared our answers in subsequent meetings. Modify it to suit your own needs!

CATEGORIES:
> **BACKGROUND**
> **EXPECTATIONS**
> **CAREER PATH**
> **TRADEOFFS**
> **ISSUES AND ENVIRONMENT**
> **ON BEING FEMALE**
> **MENTORING AND SUPPORT**
> **PAY AND REWARDS**
> **LEARNINGS**
> **OTHER**

BACKGROUND:
1) PERSONAL DATA
   a) Name (optional):
   b) Age:
   c) Profession:
   d) Education: (list all college degrees, majors, university and date received)

    e) Marital Status: (list age at marriage and duration of any marriages)

    f) Children: (list gender and age)

    g) Date entered work force:

    h) A brief summary of employment history (after HS or college) from first to most recent: (in the case of multiple jobs with one company just describe by title the first and last job). Include any breaks in employment history and state the main purpose of the break.

2) What were your parents' aspirations for you?

3) In what ways did your mother's life history influence your own choices? In what ways did your father's life history influence your choices?

4) How does your life compare to your parents' lives?

5) What was your environment like in high school? What extracurricular activities did you participate in? Were there gender differences in how girls and boys were treated or the classes they were expected to take? Were there events/experiences while you were in high school that influenced your career path? What were your views on

marriage, children, divorce, and working when you were in high school?

6) What was your environment like in college? What extracurricular activities did you participate in? Were there gender differences in how women and men were treated or the classes they were expected to take? Were there events/experiences while you were in college that influenced your career path? What were your views on marriage, children, divorce, and working when you were in college?

7) What kind of community involvement did you have in your teens? 20s? 30s? 40s?

EXPECTATIONS:

8) What were your career/life expectations (25 words or less!) going into the work force? What were they 10, 20, 30 years later? What made them change?

9) What do you think you will be doing 10, 20, 30 years from now?

CAREER PATH:

10) What were the major turning point(s) in your career?

11) At which point/stage in your career did YOU feel personally powerful for the first time?

TRADEOFFS:

12) How did your career impact your personal life? And vice versa?

13) What were the priorities in your life and what impacted them? Did these priorities change over time? Were these shared by your spouse/significant other ?

14) What factors, if any, caused you to make compromises in you life?

15) If you had to do it over again, what, if anything, would you change?

ISSUES AND ENVIRONMENT:

16) What were the major environmental factors and/or issues that influenced your career in the 60's, 70's, 80's, 90's?

17) Were there issues you encountered that frustrated you and your ability to be successful?

18) What changes would you like to see in work environment in the next 10 years?

ON BEING FEMALE:

19) Do you think being a female impacted your getting a job or how you were compensated for that job? Do you think being a female impacted your getting the jobs you have held or your ability to move forward in your career?

20) What were the biggest obstacles in the work force about being a woman? Were there benefits to being a woman in the work force?

21) Did you encounter any sexual harassment at work? How did you handle it?

22) What things about being a woman (in and out of the workplace) have changed in the last 5, 10, 20, and 30 years. What haven't? Do you feel it is easier or more difficult for women today to "have a career" compared to women 20 or 30 years ago? Why?

23) What do you most respect about the women who preceded you in your field of work? Are there things you think they did that made the workplace more or less hospitable to the women who followed them?

24) How do you see, and how did you deal with, the issues of "feminism and femininity?"

25) What best describes your role in seeking a fair work environment for all: militant; activist; politically expedient; go with the flow, anti-activist, none of the above (specify).

MENTORING AND SUPPORT:

26) What or who were the most influential forces in your life -- personal and professional?

27) Did you have strong professional relationships with others? men or women?

28) How important and how accessible have women been as mentors in your career through each decade of your career? Were they more helpful earlier in your career or later?

29) What role, if any, did you play in improving the work environment for your peers? For your successors?

PAY AND REWARDS:

30) What did you think of your starting salary? Were you making more or less (or don't know) than your male counterparts?

31) What do you think of your salary today (or when you left the work force)?

32) Did you make more or less than your spouse/partner? How did you deal with the differences? If you are married, how did you and your spouse deal with financial matters? Separate or shared bank accounts? Shared or allocated expenses?

33) What significance does money have for you emotionally (e.g., independence, security, achievement, recognition, control, other (specify))?

LEARNINGS:

34) Describe the major transitions points in your career from the perspective of growing and learning?

35) What is the message that you would pass on to the generations of women coming after you?

36) What were the key lessons you personally learned over your career? What are the key lessons you believe your generation experienced?

Authors On Authors

IN THE CORNER OFFICE

Margaret Ann Chappell joined Bell Laboratories in 1980. She spent most of her career using her technical and communication skills to identify ways new technologies could solve customer needs. She was an integral part of both the marketing and technical teams as they built leading edge products and services to enhance customers' communications. This included bringing video capabilities to a variety of devices such as ATMs, computers, and telephones. She was one of the first people in AT&T to work on products that would allow customers to make phone calls over the internet – a fairly common practice today but a radical idea in the mid-1990s. In 1993 she was appointed a Distinguished

Member of the Technical Staff at Bell Laboratories for her sustained history of outstanding technical accomplishments and leadership. Prior to joining Bell Laboratories Margaret Ann taught Psychology at Emory University and was a Post-Doctoral Fellow at Duke University. She received a B.S. from Denison University and an M.S. and Ph.D. in Psychology from Emory University.

BEYOND THE CORNER OFFICE

My seeing has improved dramatically over the past two years – although I feel like a child and am continuously amazed at the new world that is unfolding before me. Since beginning to immerse myself in photography, the world has been dramatically transformed. Details and patterns and lines and colors all jump out now. And light. How I managed to not see how subtle changes in light impact moods and feelings – both in everyday life and photography – now astounds me. Golden light is my favorite.

Photography is complementary to the things I most enjoy – family, learning, travel, and nature. I haven't quite figured out how it complements the joy of cooking – but I'm sure the connection is there somewhere. Photography has proven to be a terrific medium to bring joy to people – a perpetual goal of mine.

IN THE CORNER OFFICE

Dana Dunn earned a B.S. in mathematics from Southern Illinois University in 1972 and an M.S. in computer science from Northwestern University in 1976. In 1984, she completed the Sloan Fellows program at Massachusetts Institute of Technology, receiving an M.S. in business management. Dana began her career with AT&T in 1972 at Bell Laboratories where she managed technical development groups. While at AT&T she had a wide range of management responsibilities including application software development, product management, marketing, strategy, new business development, and operations. In 1992, she became Vice President and Chief Technical Officer for AT&T's Consumer Customer Service (Long Distance) organization. She joined Business Communication Systems in 1994, which later became part of Lucent Technologies, as Vice President of Large Business Systems. In the spring of 2000, she led the strategic negotiations for the sale of a business that culminated in establishing the largest indirect sales channel serving small and mid-sized businesses in the US. She then led a team in the successful spin off of Avaya from Lucent Technologies in 2001. Dana ended her career as the Vice President of Avaya US Services business. She was selected to serve on the Board of Governors of the Society of Sloan Fellows and currently serves on the Board of Directors of Advanta Corporation. She is also noted in the 1987 issue of Who's Who in Professional and Executive Women. Today she lives with her husband and son in Mountain Lakes, NJ.

BEYOND THE CORNER OFFICE

Since my retirement in 2001 from corporate life, most recently Avaya, I am like a sponge. A sponge in the sea lives like an animated filter, constantly straining out minute organisms that pass through its body. I involve myself in painting, photography, stained glass, needlework, gardening, gourmet cooking, music, and healthy living, continually choosing facets that enable me to gain more insight into life's daily challenges. My goals now are to embellish life -- not just mine, but the lives of my son and husband living here in Mountain Lakes, New Jersey as well as those of my stepdaughter and grandchildren living in New Canaan, Connecticut.

Part of our learning comes from travel. My family has explored many parts of the world and we will soon live in Killarney, Ireland for one year while my son completes his eighth grade year abroad. My 29-year career in the technology field was filled with enormous learning and growth opportunities, which primarily exercised the left side of my brain. Now I have the good fortune to have the time to open up more opportunities for exploring and expanding the right side of my brain. The more I learn, the more I want to learn.

IN THE CORNER OFFICE

Fran Henig joined Bell Laboratories in 1964 and retired in 1996. She spent most of her career as a Division Manager, designing, building and deploying software systems that helped domestic and international telecommunications providers maintain their networks and run their customer service operations.

Fran is an alumna of Wheaton College, Massachusetts, and has an M.S. from Stevens Institute of Technology in Hoboken, NJ. She and her husband, Edward, have been married almost 30 years and live in Short Hills, NJ.

BEYOND THE CORNER OFFICE

My husband's friend, Jeannie, when things get tough at the office, comments "There's a reason they call it work." For me, as satisfying and intellectually stimulating as work was, it was almost always work. Retirement, on the other hand, has so far been like finding the sweet spot in the racquet, to use Pam's tennis analogy. I get to play, explore, try new things, and work hard at things (like botanical art) that have no obvious value, except to me. I get to take a walk in the middle of the day and enjoy daylight in the middle of winter. I feel like I have some balance in my life for the first time.

IN THE CORNER OFFICE

Pamela S. Hufnagel started her career in the brokerage industry as a Portfolio Analyst managing investment portfolios. In the late 80's, she moved to Germany as the Executive Director for the largest USO (United Services Organization) outside of the U.S. Pam set the standard for overseas USO operations to be financially self-sufficient. Upon returning from

Germany, Pam began her career at AT&T where she held a wide variety of management positions including Marketing, Product Management, Strategic Development, Business Planning and Operations. In her position with AT&T Broadband as VP of Market Development and Operations, her responsibilities included leading an organization to launch cable telephony across the Eastern half of the US utilizing the talents and resources of AT&T and the two cable companies AT&T purchased, TCI and Media One. Most recently, Pam is a Senior Director of Market Planning and Strategy for AT&T Wireless.

Pam earned a B.S. in marketing from Georgetown University and an MBA. from Seton Hall University. She resides in Basking Ridge, N.J., with her husband Jim and her standard poodle Bailey.

BEYOND THE CORNER OFFICE

Bounce, bounce, thwak, swoosh, plop. Since I left my last corporate job, I feel like a tennis ball. Sometimes, I'm flying smoothly in the right direction feeling like everything is going my way - swoosh. More often, I am bouncing out-of-bounds, plopping weakly over the net or being struck with such power that all control is lost. It's been an agitated and irregular flow of energy to get back in the game of getting the next interview, networking and exploring non-traditional options for my Act II. I would like to strike that illusive "ace" and not have to worry anymore about what's next and just get on with it. I'm ready for Wimbledon.

IN THE CORNER OFFICE

Carol C. Knauff is a retired Vice President from AT&T where she spent 29 years leading organizations to market place and financial success. She represented AT&T in a number of national organizations. These were: U.S.O., Council for Better Business Bureaus, and National Council of LaRaza. She is an elected member of The Pennsylvania State University Alumni Council, and was named Outstanding Engineering Alumni in 1995 and Alumni Fellow in 1998 by Penn State. She also received the Pinnacle Award in 2002 from Fairleigh Dickinson University. After retiring from AT&T, Carol was the CEO of WorldWideWeb Networxs, a NASDAQ company.

Carol received a B. S. in Electrical Engineering from Penn State in 1969, a Masters in

Engineering Management from the University of Missouri-Rolla and an MBA from Fairleigh Dickinson.

She currently resides in Mendham, NJ with her husband Jeff and their two daughters, Kathleen, 23 and Christine, 17. Carol is active in her community and volunteers many hours.

BEYOND THE CORNER OFFICE

I am a battering ram, I am. I've lived my whole life one way. Pick something hard and wonderful, and work your butt off to get it done. That approach worked for the first 53 years of my life. But, now it's not working any more. My head hurts from battering on all those solid oak doors that have yet to give an inch. Have I been picking the wrong doors? Beats me, and I'm just about out of ideas. Maybe it's time to be a wanderer.

IN THE CORNER OFFICE

Duffy Kopriva a.k.a. Margaret Kopriva graduated from the University of Pittsburgh in 1969 with a B.S. in Mathematics. She began her career as a computer programmer with AT&T in

New Jersey. Moving through AT&T's data systems, engineering and marketing departments she achieved the level of Division Manager before leaving the corporate world in 1984 to pursue her entrepreneurial dreams. She experimented with various opportunities until settling upon the business suites industry, opening her first HQ Business Center in New Jersey in 1988. A second center in New Jersey was opened several years later and the third expansion led her to Jacksonville, Florida. After nurturing the growing company for ten years, she was rewarded with a buy-out offer and she retired at the age of 50. Ms. Kopriva is currently active in environmental causes, real estate, new business ventures and provides guidance to young entrepreneurs. She lives with her husband in Jacksonville, FL and Mount Arlington, NJ.

BEYOND THE CORNER OFFICE

At 55, I still seek new ideas, new places, and new adventures. No longer spurred on by the need to make a living, the motivation is now one of self-discovery and fulfillment, more mellow and rich. I watch birds and garden, the pastimes that surely identify you as an older person. But the glory of this stage of life is that you do what pleases you, not worrying about image. Recently I took the temporary position of Chief Operating Officer for a small, but rapidly growing company, the CEO being 30 years old and the rest of the organization even younger. To my great relief, they liked having a seasoned businessperson in their midst and I liked playing the role of mentor and teacher. The experience let me relive the tremendous emotional rush that comes with action and creativity, ideas scurrying around the brain and the physical exhilaration of successful team efforts. For the artistic side of me I dabble with creative writing and botanical drawing, when I'm not on some scenic waterway kayaking and bird watching – yes it's possible to do them both at the same time. Time with my husband of twenty-five years is frequently spent on the golf course. My golf handicap is boringly high and this is one thing that sadly hasn't changed in 20 years.

IN THE CORNER OFFICE

Kathleen Meier started her corporate career in 1971 as a shareowner correspondent in the Stock and Bond Division in the Treasury Department with AT&T. She worked for AT&T for 24 years and for Lucent Technologies for 5 years. After retiring from Lucent in 2000 she accepted a position as the marketing officer for a start-up company located in Richardson Texas.

In her 32-year career, she was known as an experienced leader, most recognized for her strategic and tactical marketing savvy, but also had broad experience in Corporate Strategy, Operations, Project Management and Finance. She was an industry expert in voice processing and telecommunication with an ability to translate technology topics for non-technical audiences. She was a seasoned leader in growing new and emerging businesses and has managed businesses ranging from $10M in revenue to $500M. Her titles included Vice President of Marketing, General Manager, Director of New Business Development, and Director of Product Management. She lives with her husband, David, in Bucks County, PA.

Education:

Duke University, 1996/1997 Duke Global Executive Program

Indiana University 1988 Executive Education in Global Management

Pace University, 1982 Masters of Science (MS) Advanced Management

Rutgers University, 1968 Douglass College, BA

BEYOND THE CORNER OFFICE

I am renovating my life:

> I do a lot of soul-searching and exploration.

> I am unlearning old patterns, trying to break bad habits and learn new ones.

> This is hard work.

> I have known my husband for 34 years; I have lived in my home for 27 years, and I worked for one company for 29 years.

> The secret is to know what to treasure and keep and to clean out the old to make room for the new.

> *This will take time. I have new dreams to fulfill and in time a new life will emerge.*

IN THE CORNER OFFICE

Judith Scheffler received BS degrees in Technical Writing and Electrical Engineering from Carnegie Mellon. In 1965 she joined AT&T Bell Laboratories and subsequently earned an MS degree in Computer Science from Stevens Institute of Technology. By 1971, already the mother of two daughters, she became one of the first female supervisors at Bell Laboratories. In 1989 she was promoted to an executive position at

AT&T. She was the Chief Information Officer of one of the larger business units at Lucent Technologies when she took early retirement in 1998. She is listed in "Who's Who in Information Technology 1998-1999 and 1999-2000.

Today she lives with her husband in Summit, NJ, developing a second career in creative nonfiction. She has a column in her local newspaper in New Jersey and is also writing essays for a newspaper in Rangeley, Maine.

BEYOND THE CORNER OFFICE

I am a nomad. Sometimes I think of my life like those maps in the center of airline magazines. Heavily drawn arcs leave my home in New Jersey. They go to Boston where my doctor daughter (Kathryn) lives across from the arboretum with her husband and one-year-old son, to Santa Fe where my writer daughter (Elizabeth) lives with her little white dog in a cocita (small house) on a hill above an arroyo, and to a remote part of Western Maine where my log cabin sits in a spruce-balsam forest that edges a lake. Thinner arcs go from my suburban home to Cape Hatteras where my brother and his wife (previously my college roommate) have a vacation house on stilts above the dunes, to Chesterfield, Virginia and Elkton, Maryland where my stepdaughters and their children live, and to the French countryside where my husband and I like to visit. Wherever I go, I carry a soft-covered notebook so I can write my musings about the strange and wonderful way that a life evolves.

IN THE CORNER OFFICE

Yvonne Shepard started her career at AT&T Bell Laboratories in 1968. In the first decade of her career she developed software for computer Operating Systems and Data Networks; during the second decade she participated and led projects with increasing responsibilities in the areas of Marketing, Operations, and Strategy and Business Planning; during the third decade as President and COO of ATT of Puerto Rico and Marketing Vice-President for Global Markets she led major units of ATT to market growth and profitability. After retiring from ATT in 1999, she started a consulting business where she is actively involved in helping companies to profitably market their products and services in the US and in Latin America. She has a B.A. in Mathematics from St. Mary-of-the-Woods College, an M.S in Computer Science from Northwestern University, and an M.S. in Business from Pace University.

She is married to Ronald Zanders and they reside in Flemington, NJ.

BEYOND THE CORNER OFFICE

Since 9/11 I have become deeply aware that life is a treasure and that time is too precious to be squandered. So I am going for it -- I am learning, I am supporting, I am experiencing, I am working, I am redecorating, I am gardening, I am reconnecting with old friends, I am teaching, I am staying fit, I am caring, and I am growing. And this is the way it will be.

I no longer wear the business attire I felt I had to have - a Knight's armor suit! This I have shed. I am one in thought, action and feelings.

Credits

Hands (in *The Baby Belles in Act II*):
   photograph by Fran Henig
Copy of Picasso's Stravinsky (in *In the Beginning*):
   Yvonne Shepard
The Pub at Blackhorse Tavern (in *Remembering You*):
   photograph by Carol Knauff
Lyrics (in *Remembering You*): "I Will Remember You"
   by Sarah McLachlan, Seamus Egan and Dave
   Merenda, 1999
Pink Dogwood (in *New Directions*):
   Graphite sketch by Fran Henig
Bailey, The Poodle (in *Hanging out with Older People*):
   photograph by Pam Hufnagel
Flower (in *I Am My Father's Daughter*):
   photograph by Margaret Ann Chappell
Grilled Clam Recipe (in *A Diagnosis*):
   Dana Dunn (adapted from Martha Stewart)
Long Beach Island (in *Fulfilling Dreams*):
   photograph by Kathy Meier
Kayaks (in *An Adventuress on the Hunt*):
   photograph by Duffy Kopriva
Fire Island Walk (in *Summary*):
   photograph by Fran Henig
Rear View Mirror (in *Resources*):
   photograph by Fran Henig
Cover Design: Fran Henig
Cover Photograph: Margaret Ann Chappell